CHASING
SHADOWS

Richard D'Arcy swears that he was intoxicated by the waft of
'Brasso' in that clean, clear Torbay air. He and Jonny had crossed
the championship fleet close-hauled, on the wind, in preparation for
their final tack onto starboard, and the glory of the finishing line. He
had even started to prepare his winning speech.

T.N. JOBLING

First published May 2014 by

THOMAS JOBLING
Co. Antrim BT40 1BP

© Text, Thomas Jobling, 2014
© Sketches, Thomas Jobling, 2014

For information on ordering and availability, contact the author at
tn.jobling@gmail.com.

A CIP catalogue record for this book is available from the British
Library.

ISBN   978-1-29186952-1

George

I hope that you get as
much fun reading, as I get
in creating it

Thomas Jolly

Nov 2014

Acknowledgements

In completing this my debut novel I am reminded of the various people who have pushed, inspired coached and guided me along the way. Two people come to mind immediately: Champion sailor Paul Rowan who 'mugged' me into taking over his sailing column in the local paper so many, many years ago. Gullible? Yes I certainly was, but it was a first step. WM Nixon, the renowned yachting columnist and author, thereafter became my guide. He coached me in my embryo world of yachting journalism. Without these two gentlemen I doubt, I wonder, if my nautical scribbling would have ever seen the light of day. That was some forty years ago...

In terms of 'Chasing Shadows' the journey, although frustrating at times, has been exciting and fulfilling. Again I need to spotlight some folk politely standing in the shadows: Ruth Carr, poet and writer at the Crescent Arts Centre, Belfast has been an inspiration to me.

Martin Tyrrell at Queens University assisted with prose techniques and focused me on the mechanics of fiction writing, while Michael Faulkner (mikefaulkner@elite.co.uk) has been my proofing guru. Andrew of Finch Creative Design produced the cover and my gratitude is also directed at the Larne Writers' Group, Gary Ferguson in particular, (larnewrtitersgroup.com) of which I am a proud member. They inspire, critique, and assist – a truly great bunch of people.

Of course, without the patience and support of my lovely understanding wife Jane, and the family circle, 'Chasing Shadows' would have remained folded away in a darkened drawer.

Thinking of you Stan...

Preface

This novel is set in the late sixties early seventies. Richard D'Arcy a north-of-England lad in his early twenties, is on one hand, consumed with the eccentricities of the period; the music the fashion and happy-go-lucky attitudes, while on the other, he is driven.

He is propelled by ambitions of success and fame. A chance meeting with Jonny Dubois acted as a catalyst. It helped turn his dream into a reality. This is Richard's story. It charts his journey through three life channels: sporting achievement, development of life-long and life changing friendships, and how he acquired success in the world of business – from office junior to managing director.

From a sporting perspective this is not the stereotypical goalmouth struggle. This is the ultimate tale of success on the waves... It describes in detail, from regatta to regatta, from race to race in intricate detail how D'Arcy & Dubois launched their challenge from novice 'pond' sailors to claim the coveted national sailing crown.

Chapter one opens with an elderly Richard D'Arcy reminiscing of his victories past. He is on board his daughter's yacht. It is near noon on a baking regatta day. Taking to relative coolness of the cabin he recaptures his life; he remembers not only his catalogue of sail-boat successes and the life he shared with Samantha, but also his life-long friend Jonny, among others.

Richard's relationship with Jonny develops and deepens as they challenge the world of competitive sailing. But this is amply balanced with their shore-side activities as they stagger through various indiscretions – mostly Richards. They party, enjoy music and of course, chase young ladies... While Jonny is a student of density and is articulate tall and fit Richard is a factory worker, a junior buyer with a tendency to allow his mouth to open prior to engaging his brain. Gaffs and apologies litter this tale. Such a gaff almost scuppered a chance encounter with 'a posh blond'. It was one of those frozen in aspic moments; Richard was instantly smitten but soon realised that she, Samantha, was way out of his league.

He however was convinced that there had been a spark. After what seemed like an eternity they met again; but the new meeting coincided with the most important event in the boys sporting career. It was the national championship and the last thing they needed was a romantic diversion. They were seriously chasing titles now, not shadows.

Time had rubbed away the sparse knowledge of Samantha's background. He still fancied her; he just knew that they were meant for each other and something told him that she held the same view.

Finally, and after a week of untapped opportunities, romance finally blossomed. But it was on the eve of the final race in the series. As they pulled away from that starting line, in that most crucial of races, Richard remained locked in love's lust. His concentration was not what it needed to be!

The outcome and the reverberations of that day set up a catalogue of events that would restructure Richard D'Arcy's life-path—both for the good, and the dire...

CHASING SHADOWS

Note: A glossary of terms (sailing speak) can be found on page 325

Warning: This book contains strong language, and text of a sexual nature

Chapter One

Drifting

A fickle wind ghosted *Mistress* across Torbay. Barely two knots registered on her electronic log. Clouds hung over the racecourse like wisps in the azure sky.

Lapping wavelets hypnotised Richard D'Arcy as he reclined against a leeward cockpit. He was soaking up the late morning sun. This was serenity, he thought. He was, of course, fully aware of the tension building among the seven-strong crew.

From under the brim of a battered Tilley hat Richard kept a keen eye on on-deck activities. He was no passenger. His role on the yacht was that of tactician and mentor. Now in his advancing years, Richard had achieved plenty and amassed a mountain of experience in his fifty years of competitive sailing. This was his daughter and son-in-law's yacht, and they seemed delighted to finally have him on board. He too was content with the arrangement. And although he was working hard to appear calm, within him a heady rush of excitement and competitive spirit was rekindling. He itched to reach across, to take control of the wheel… Just to touch it.

The clouds moved lightly. He looked beyond the glassy seascape for signs of a new breeze. The watery metronome, however, was pulling him further into a midday doze, his eyelids drooping in the warmth, his back massaged by the motion of the yacht.

Hat tilted over brow, his head and shoulders were positioned bolt upright. A statue-like and well-practiced posture designed to hide any hint of his slumbers. It promised to be a long day afloat. The conditions suggested a crawl of a race. Richard remembered clearly a previous encounter of many seasons past. It had played out dramatically on these very waters; the outcome, he would never forget. Nor the aftermath, which influenced, nay reshaped, his life.

Onboard, the crew remained still. Any hasty movement could rustle the whispers of available breeze out of their sloth-like spinnaker. Balmy conditions demanded concentration. Inevitably, an air of frustration had begun to build, not least with the skipper. In a careless moment she voiced her irritation.

'Wind, bloody wind. Where is it when you need it? Oh this is hopeless.'

Aware of the developing situation, Richard had spent too many seasons in competition to ignore the negativity into which crews can lapse. He was concerned, and he reported his observations and suggestions directly to his daughter, the skipper, while at the same time administering a parental calming touch.

'Easy Susie, let the boat do the work. Look, we're moving along steadily; slow, but steady. Everyone and every yacht, is experiencing the same conditions. The secret is to watch the wind, watch it move and shift. Remember how I taught you. Remember your little dinghy all those years ago?' She smiled and immediately her vice-like grip on the big wheel loosened. The boat, it almost seemed, surged forward…

Susanna was Richard's youngest, and like her father was an accomplished sailor. In fact she was defending her title. This was a new yacht – a different package altogether from her previous and successful 22-footer. *Mistress* was eleven feet longer and much more powerful, though in these conditions she felt the opposite. It was the final race of Regatta Week and the crew, who had quietly modified the yacht's name from *Mistress,* to *Mistress of Mayhem*, were again in the running for silverware. At this moment the odds were stacked against them, but there was a long way to go. The finish was hours away. They needed this result.

With the nervous staring eased and an onboard camaraderie restored, Richard, lost in the stillness of the day, mentored no more. Flashbacks of an earlier time washed over his heavy eyes – his successes and his failures, the highs and the lows.

He saw himself growing from spotty youth to eloquent champion of the high seas; from Eleven Plus failure to main board director. The twin threads of his reminiscing, though, were the absolute love of his life, Samantha, and of course his lifelong pal Jonny Dubois, whom he first met on a snow-draped Saturday evening back in the very early seventies.

Little did his daughter, or any of the crew, know the extent to which this outing was providing him with a crucial brick of support in his emerging from a darkness he had been battling for years.

Chapter Two

Choice Acquaintance

Richard D'Arcy and Jonny Dubois sort of crashed into each other.
The meeting place was a once grotty pub, on the outskirts of
Oldcastle Newtown. Richard, bursting through the narrow swing
doors to escape the bite of an unseasonal snowstorm, caught Jonny's
shoulder as he cleared away the tea-time glassware from tightly
packed tables. Richard was an infrequent weekend drinker there. He
was an after-work-pint man. He was also a member of the pub's
quiz team; the music man and, if he did say so himself, the nautical
expert. He'd never come across big Jonny before.

Apologies offered and accepted, Richard proceeded to disrobe.
First, off came the camel duffle coat. Then a crust of snow
transferred itself neatly from hood to cleared table.

'Oh shit, sorry mate. Hey I'm Richard. Richard D'Arcy. Haven't seen you before I don't think?.'

'Jonathan Dubois, Jonny.' An outstretched hand found Richard a willing recipient.

'No. I'm the Friday to Sunday relief. Worked here for a few months now. Used to stay up in Brummie but hated the bar there. The manager was a right old witch. So when this vacancy appeared I jumped at it. Also means I get to see my folks on a weekend basis. Yeah, it's good. Anyway, what can I get you?'

'Pint of Whatney's please, mate.' Richard's voice was muffled due to the unwinding of his purple and yellow LSE scarf, and the heckling of regulars.

'Sorry, didn't catch that; pint of...?'

'Watneys.'.

It was a performance in itself. In response to the wisecracks Richard remarked with a smile:

'If it's good enough for Jagger, it's good enough for me.'

His sodden flares drained unnoticed into puddles. Trickles of water like tributaries followed the worn grouting of the granite-slabbed floor. The roar of the stacked coal fire soon sparked life back into numbed fingers and toes. The room glowed, and any hint of damp soon evaporated. The old bar was cosy. Smoke from the fire and countless cigarettes had re-yellowed the low ceiling.

The Cellars, not long restored, was a lively meeting place, yet it retained its quaintness. The clientele covered a broad mix of age and class and, of course, storytelling. It was more than just a local: it was a social club, educational dug-out and, until last orders at least, a cross-community project for the distressed and homeless.

Richard took a generous sup. Then he sat the branded glass tankard back on the counter and repositioned himself on a somewhat rickety bar stool. He pulled the latest *Practical Boat Owner* from the inside pocket of the duffle coat. A coat which now draped the adjacent stool next to the fire. While flicking the pages, he also reopened the conversation with the barman. He, in turn, stole a few glances at the magazine while dispensing orders at the pumps.

'Ah, nothing like a cool pint to warm you on a bleak autumn night.'

'Yeah I know, it's really stupid, but it does have that affect.'

'You havin' one yourself?'

'Na, not while I'm working. Might have one afterwards, we'll see.' A conversation had developed. Gradually it took on a pace but just as quickly evaporated. The place had filled up and the pulling of pints and pushing of optics had moved up a pace too.

They had hit it off straight away. Jonny was supplementing his student grant with bar work. His evening's shift completed, he and Richard set out to investigate whatever entertainment opportunities an uptown Saturday night offered.

Standing a smidgen over six feet, Jonny was a good four, maybe five inches taller than Richard. That he was some three years younger was not evident. He was a student of dentistry at the

Birmingham university. Behind a smokescreen of maturity, young Dubois would unhitch his weekday student credentials prior to bar work. The job augmented his finances, and at the same time offered him an 'educational' fillip – his aging clientele could always be relied on to provide him with worldly advice.

Whether it was his considerable stature or his assertive manner of speaking, he certainly displayed a command of that bar. He oversaw the Friday darts night, dispensed drink fluidly – three pints filling simultaneously– and he could deal with the Saturday night drunk firmly yet with sympathy: Jonny Dubois was a management gift for the owners, Bob and Sandra Hepworth.

He was smart – academically – but also down to earth. People took to him. Richard D'Arcy was no exception. But whilst young Dubois was the weekend face of the pub, behind his friendly persona he was particular in his choice of acquaintance. He was especially cautious of those acquired from across a beer-stained and cigarette-burnt oak counter. Richard D'Arcy was therefore an exception.

Jonny was heavily into his sport: rugby, soccer – especially Aston Villa FC – cars and rowing. If Jonny was honest, though, the rowing was but an inherited regime from his grammar school days. He nevertheless carried the skill seamlessly through to his university leisure. He liked boats and enjoyed competition, but he was equally happy to absorb the wildlife of the river bank.

His rugged good looks and luminous blue eyes acted like neon – he was not without his admirers, male as well as female.

Whilst he undoubtedly could, and surely would, have got away with it, he was far from flamboyant. If anything, he was the opposite. He always remained conscious of his presence and his natural attraction to the opposite sex, at least in sobriety.

He was also well aware that in the rough and tumble of chatting up young ladies this presence could manifest itself as the target of male aggression. Having an able sidekick on hand as he strutted around the clubs, pubs and dancehalls was a key consideration.

Richard, however, weighing in at some 10½ stone, was no advertisement for the body beautiful. Neither skinny nor obese he considered himself adequately fit... for watching soccer. He never really played much sport, considered it to be far too energetic. More importantly, he didn't enjoy getting kicked or the prospect of sliding in spit. Richard was a tough enough cookie though, streetwise and well able to look after himself.

His overriding indulgence was music; his overriding musical influences were Hendrix, Free, the 'Stones (as opposed to the Beatles) and Atlantic soul. Then there were cars and needless to say, young ladies, the chasing of... These activities absorbed a major portion of his day, every day. But significantly, perhaps oddly, he also had another passion – for all things afloat. Considering that his home – indeed his upbringing – were many miles inland, this stood out as a curious interest. From whence it came, no-one, especially Richard, was sure…

Richard was undeniably a handsome chap; pale in complexion, with strong eyebrows looking down on a finely sculpted nose. Porcelain teeth were set in rows of perfection. He looked younger than his 20-odd years; boyish almost. This could work for or against him, both in the workplace and out on the town. One particularly embarrassing moment would haunt him for years…

Today, the memory was powerful enough to nudge Richard back into semi-consciousness. He quickly checked whether anyone had witnessed the upward jerk of his head, but he seemed to have got away with it. With an air of aged dreaminess, he used the moment to check on his daughter's progress. A skyward glance found a spinnaker now maximising what had become a gentle breeze. He was satisfied that all was well. Well enough to allow him to retreat to the luxury and relative coolness of the main cabin. The overhead sun was reflecting off the pale deck, and reflection from the rippled sea conspired to magnify the effect. It was baking. He asked if all the crew had adequate sun block applied, then turned quietly to his daughter.

'Wake me if you need me, Darling.'

He offered up one of his wry smiles and finally disappeared down the companionway to take up station on the starboard bunk. The softness of the upholstery provided him with a luxurious sump.

It prompted a rapid return to a state of reminiscence and the events of that Manchester outing, so many years ago.

His mouth smiled, his eyes became heavy, and he saw himself again: a young D'Arcy in the final furlong of chatting up an obviously older but, seductively attractive lady. She reached towards him. He readied himself for her gentle caress. With thumb and forefinger she pinched his cheek, planting a mummy-like kiss on his forehead and remarking:

'Oh duck, you're a lovely boy.'

And then she waltzed out of the club on the arm of her friend. Both were smirking. The only consolations were that the place was dimly lit, it was late, and there were few if any witnesses.

In the work place, too, his impish looks would do him few favours. This would become evident when he was sent onto the shop floor, where he had used a natural ability to think on his feet, to communicate out of tricky situations. It was his guide and ally in the ways of the working world.

As in any factory environment with a predominately female work-force, in the days preceding a holiday shut-down – especially for Christmas – life for a 'pretty boy' could be perilous, if a chap was unprepared. Shop floor education was raw. It was swift, and it could be life-changing, making the raunchiest of office parties look tame.

Richard was, or became, extremely able in his dealings with the opposite sex at work. But interestingly, over the years from office junior to management, serious liaisons with colleagues and co-workers were few and far between. Interspersed with 'uptown' clubbing and pubbing duties, sometimes he would mix at the factory social club, especially when funds were low – the drink was cheap. He drifted in and out of various societies; they held meetings at the facilities the club offered. He would join up for the occasional cabaret night, but always – generally – Richard erected a polite screen between himself and most of his colleagues. He was instructed at the start of his working life – by whom he could not remember – never to mix business with pleasure. In his career quest it was a mantra he held close: 'Colleagues are just that – colleagues. Not friends, generally.'

Fashion and dressing in sync with the style of the day was crucial in his post-work world. Although his build was not in Jonny's league, clothes nevertheless hung well on him. Platforms offered him an extra inch or so of much sought-after height. This, together with an affable quality, afforded Richard D'Arcy the tag of 'a good catch'.

Music, socialising and ladies – not necessarily in that order – were to become the boys' common bond. It was the catalyst in their emerging friendship. While Jonny flexed his physique Richard's tales of aquatic brilliance came to the rescue of many a failed chat-up line. It was true – at least in his mind – that all the hot girls love a sailor. That's what he told his workmates. This was his invariable defence when they goaded him about messing about in girly boats. They would rather he was taking part in the Sunday morning league.

At that time he had a fairly rough old second-hand sailing dinghy. The nearby boating and fishing lake was where he would sail it. He would win the occasional club race. It was all very sporadic. His dinghy not being 'single-handed', Richard always needed to recruit someone to act as crew for those races. To achieve this collaboration the usual pre-Sunday round of telephone calls was required. He would frequently bemoan his lot. He was in the wrong business. He should be running a recruitment agency. But his sweet-talking normally produced a result – more often than not, female. His sailing was his interest. It verged on a passion. His persistence paradoxically made him one of the regular participants at the club. He became quite successful. But that recurring weekend pattern was wearing him down. Recruitment frustrations and a catalogue of cancellations and no-shows were testing him.

However, a lively breeze, crackling sails and the rustle of the tree-lined banks of the Long Lake always injected life back into his nautical endeavours. His favourite time for sailing was in the windy autumn. A frosted shoreline exploded in a canvas of reds and orange contrasting with menacing black water, caped with silver streams of spindrift. It was an exhilarating time. Even if sailing was not possible, the magnificence of it all was uplifting enough. He could sit on his parked dinghy and lose himself in the vista, while relishing just how much his 'hecklers' were missing.

He was also an avid reader of nautical publications. His material ranged from *Sea Breezes* to *Yachting World*. He enjoyed nothing more than to park himself privately and drown within the pages of the specialist magazines. This choice of reading material would, he was convinced, someday assist in the furthering of his understanding of the finer elements of competitive sailing. He would frequently align his outings on the lake to those detailed in national race reports. Occasionally, in moments of extreme boredom, the name Richard D'Arcy would be superimposed onto a winner's rostrum...

OK, he would reassure himself, everyone is allowed to dream. With Richard, though, there was the embryo of a burning ambition behind his dreams. His day would come, he determined. He craved fame, recognition at least. His knowledge base had expanded – he could certainly talk a good race. The big issue however was in translating this acquired theory into practice. His sailing in reality was haphazard. It was seat-of-the-pants stuff. Richard could never get commitment from the gaggle of people to whom he had introduced the pleasures. Equally, any travel into the outside world of yachting, which he craved and avidly read about, was not even on the horizon.

Travel to a neighbouring club's regatta, however, was a possibility. But without an associate to act as crew, it wasn't even on the schedule. In truth there was no schedule. It was probably akin to the 'small town – big-timer' syndrome. But the more he read those 'travellers' tales' the more he wanted a slice of the action. It was abundantly clear that he needed a cohort. He craved someone who could commit. He reasoned that there must be someone who shared similar ambitions. But that someone needed to have an inbuilt ability to understand and digest the complexities of his chosen sport.

So, several beers and a handful of Bacardi & Cokes later, the Jonny boy had agreed to ditch his oars in favour of a Sunday afternoon to sample some sailing. Since meeting Jonny Dubois that autumn night, Richard had sensed that he might just have found his perfect partner. Richard was excited but apprehensive; could it all be too good to be true?

After that introduction to sailing, contact between them fizzled. More than a month passed before they bumped into each other again. It happened at a midweek party in a club, uptown in Birmingham.

Richard was 'supporting' a friend at a stag night session while Jonny had joined an end-of-shift hospital outing. After several 'getting-to-know-you-again' Bacardi's and… yeah, they were ready to launch their own America's Cup campaign!

It took most of the early season for Richard and Jonny to gel. Jonny's ability to understand the rudiments and indeed the mechanics of sailing impressed. His sure-footedness and fitness provided Richard, the helmsman, with the luxury of being able to concentrate fully on the complexities of actually sailing a sailboat efficiently. This was especially so in windier conditions. Fairly quickly, they were competing for club prizes and indeed, by a whisker, ended their first season together as runners-up. This was not a bad return for one year's teamwork, they concluded, in a moment of self-congratulation.

Another commotion on deck roused Richard from his siesta. Popping his head out of the companionway he quickly figured that the wind, what there was of it, had changed direction. It had necessitated a sail change – hence, the commotion. The final folds of the multi-coloured spinnaker were disappearing down the forward hatch. The replacement white sail was being trimmed. Squinting up into the blinding sun, Richard again took stock of conditions. After a few moments he quietly advised his daughter of a building cloud base way over towards Weymouth. He suggested that that the lightweight spinnaker be re-packed and made ready for re-hoisting. Taking a further look around the racecourse he added:

'Umm, don't forget about the tide bending round that headland, Dear.'

He directed his daughter's attention towards the shoreline.

'I'll come up and have a wee look later.'

He knew the eccentricities of the bay like the elderly markings on the back of his hand. She nodded quietly wiped her brow and with a frustrated whisper replied:

'Yes father.'

There was tenseness in her voice. Richard pretended not to notice. He thought better of overshadowing her. Instead he returned to the more bearable temperature of the cabin. His competitive instincts were aroused. He felt good. It had been a long time since a smile came so easily to his gnarled and shadowed face. But he needed to reopen his mental memoir; it was addictive. No notion that he might be neglecting his above-deck duties was considered.

Father had total confidence in daughter's ability; certainly more than Susanna had of her own. Repositioning himself on the navy and cream striped upholstery, Richard took up where he had left off… A new season was beckoning.

A New Year and new season; the D'Arcy-Dubois confidence he remembered had remained high. They had re-launched their much-loved 'mistress' after a winter's titillation. She was freshly painted in new colours. Now signal box red with a white cove line, she looked fresh and sharp.

Immediately, they carried on where they had left off. So, in due course, to their first away fixture! This was the moment that Richard had been striving for. It represented the first objective in his campaign for fame. He was excited. He was running around organising, reorganising. He was a being a complete pain in the arse. At home and around the club, it was the same. His father

Arthur eventually calmed him; his reference to a headless chicken seemed to do the trick.

Father and son sat down to unravel Richard's tangle. A focus was needed. Although the venue was only a few short miles away it was his first time. The journey would be a challenge in itself, never mind the regatta. Arthur also commented, with a smidgen of sarcasm, on the fact that his partner Jonny was obviously no fool. He had remained, perhaps wisely, in his Birmingham halls of residence. He was well out of it, well away from the hothouse, Arthur thought quietly, and smiled.

There was a turmoil rising within Richard's half-conscious recall. A certain1975 national sailing championship flashed large. The memory was strong, strong enough to override dreams of inaugural regattas; strong enough to make him stir. Suddenly, he was catapulted right back to that same championship challenge which took place on the water on which he was again competing. More especially, and in vivid Technicolor, he was reliving that final drive for the ultimate title; how could he forget?

To this day Richard D'Arcy swears he was intoxicated by the waft of 'Brasso' in that clean, clear Torbay air. He and Jonny crossed the fleet close-hauled on the wind in preparation for the final tack onto starboard, and the glory of the finishing line. He had even started to prepare his winning speech.

They glanced at, and mentally measured, the distance on the second-placed boat as she passed under their stern. Then, following to the letter their automatic and systematic check for anything in their boat that could snag, foul or jam, Richard called:

'Ready about.'

He pushed the tiller away.

Their craft, aptly named *Satisfaction*, sharply rounded up, to be perfectly positioned to the windward of Simms & Prendergast, the favourites.

They both knew that there was no way back for John & Julian. With adrenalin levels at maximum and with a shared smile, they were content that it was in the bag. It was a dream no more. Their first ever national title was within a whisker of reality...

Eyes open, he found himself staring, with quickened breath, up at the deck-head. He was enveloped in a cold sweat. There followed a quiet reflection. It was enough time to calm his breathing, to ease the pounding within his chest and allow a further gathering of his thoughts and his bearings.

He remembered only too well how that race concluded! He also wondered: what if a different path had been trodden, how different could his life have been? It would surely have been a life trodden in the company of others?

Whether it would it have been rewarded with such riches, he would never know. Whether the lifelong friendship with Jonny, and indeed with Dave Gilmore, would have happened is questionable. Certainly, his relationship with Samantha would not have materialised!

He finally smiled a contented smile. Returning his head to the bunk, his eyelids once more flickered, heavy. He contented himself with the knowledge that the decision to venture into the 'outside world' of sailing was a definite life-changer. The memory and the detail of that inaugural regatta quickly returned. He slipped back into a luxurious sleep; this time, however, it was long, deep and sound.

Chapter Three

New Directions

After the first day of their first ever regatta, dreams of success and stardom lay in tatters. They seriously considered whether they should cut their losses, and slink away. But that would mean forfeiting not only the enormous cost of their half-decent B&B, but also the post-race entertainment – an excellent local blues band. So many decisions! It didn't take them long to agree that quitting was not an option. Nothing to do with money of course. Having done a quick recce and considered the talent pool, they simply concluded that their expertise could be directed more effectively in other quarters. It would be rude to leave.

Their state of deflation and despondency following the first day's sailing had, unbeknown to them, been transmitted to a wider audience. En route to the changing room, a few of the lads against whom they had just sailed introduced themselves. Dave Gilmore, Michael Murphy, Julian Prendergast. Conversations developed.

The crux appeared to be that whilst their opening performances had been capable, their pace faded, and oh so quickly – a recurring pattern in each of the races sailed that day. As Julian gently pointed out, their little craft was probably better suited to pottering than to racing. Then, with one voice, the group proceeded to explain why.

By regatta standards, they had sailed quite well … in parts. Their newfound 'advisors' decreed that they were especially strong pulling away from each of the starts. As new faces, they got themselves noticed at the first turning marker. That was the positive. But for the boys it led inexorably to a joint pronouncement.

'It was just that — well, we seemed to get slower and slower as each and every race ran its course; perhaps Julian was right.' Richard continued: 'Our technique was pretty crap to be honest, particularly when we found ourselves abreast of a hotshot or two.' Jonny nodded in agreement, but he summed up on a positive note.

'If nothing else, Rich, at least we gave it a go. And we learned a few things.'

Handed a lifeline of encouragement, washed, dressed and back in their civvies, they felt a degree of confidence returning to their being. Looking around the packed clubhouse and casting a discerning eye across the gathering, they turned to each other in unison; but it was Richard who said the obvious.

'Why would a mother allow her lad out of doors dressed like, well... their It's the nineteen seventies for heaven's sake, you'd think they'd have at least a little thread of fashion sense?'

'Jonny, I've just had a thought. If we start to get really good at this sailing lark we can lower our sartorial standards, try it the sailor way.' Jonny just looked at him. 'I think we need to take to the drink, mate.'

It was a Saturday evening so it must be party time. Richard, now in platforms, had boosted his height to nearer 5ft.8 inches. Cream hipster flares trailing the floor and a burnt red mandarin collared shirt acted as a beacon for incoming babes. He modelled himself on the great Dave Clark, believing there was a facial resemblance – *Richard*, he sometimes told himself, *you are one good-looking guy.* He reasoned that twinning with a suitable pop star could only embellish his appeal to the opposite sex.

Jonny was equally well turned out. His wet hair touched the collar of a nautical-styled blue and white striped t-shirt, which hung loosely out over blue denims, his ample chest ensuring an absence of midriff paunch. It was his summer castaway look.

And then there were three. Julian blew them both out of the water. He had chosen the 'Small Faces' look. His centre parting, combined with a modicum of back-combing, seemed to emphasise a pointy head, his ears just emerging from behind generous sideboards.

'A nautical Rod Stewart' was the D'Arcy-Dubois opinion: they both smiled. They nodded and agreed that there was hope for the sailing community yet. Female fashion, they all concurred, was bang up to date and, full-on: miniskirts, hipsters and hot pants. There was a sufficiency of hot babes in here tonight, and all three of the boys were up for it. As the evening wore on, however, Richard had to admit that he was off his stride. Bearing heavily was the knowledge that if he and Jonny were to stand any chance of gaining fame on the racecourse, they needed to raise finance; but how? Other than the extra income he generated from his small-time music management and dance promotions side-line, he had no immediate treasure chest, or indeed friendly bank manager.

He was staring down a darkening tunnel. As he hovered over his lifeless pint, a shaft of social light sparked him back into the moment. Coincidently, he and his bar stool found themselves positioned in the desirable company of not one, but three females. He dutifully, and with appropriate haste, discarded his financial burden.

Like silk, he moulded himself expertly into their company: a vampish brunette, a rather lovely but posh-looking blond, and an excitable redhead. Of this group, he reckoned that his fortune lay with the heavily made-up and busty brunette. The other two, desirable as they were, seemed more consumed with their own company – perhaps, he reasoned, they were in committed relationships. And so the chase was on…

The evening was convivial. Conversation flowed, music played and the dance floor provided opportunities for bravado. She, the brunette, was obviously so enamoured of him, his moves, and his infamous tales of the ocean wave that she… went off with her two girlfriends towards the end of the night. So much for all those well-intentioned drinks. *Oh, well, tomorrow is another day.* He did, however, get an apologetic smile and what he took as a personalised wave, from the blonde.

Over breakfast at their B&B, they debriefed on their day and the après-sail. *I'll need to chase that lovely lady up*, Richard promised himself. Later, he discovered that Johnny had struck gold with a girl called Penny. She was an art student who, as it turned out, was also into her sailing. Although not competing at this particular regatta, importantly she had partnered one of the leading sailors on another racing circuit. Better still, they actually won races. Neither of them knew whether Julian had clicked… Passing comment on Jonny's accomplishment, Richard was especially complimentary, albeit with a hint of sarcasm.

'She sounds a real beauty, far too good for you, Jonny Boy.'

Penny was indeed beautiful; about five foot seven – higher in heels – most of her height seemed accounted for by her legs. Her cropped brownish hair was combed forward, framing high cheek bones which emphasised her cat-like brown eyes.

In the end they stayed for the second day's racing but came ashore early from the final race. Their performance, while a little more polished than Saturday's, again did not match their expectations. And so, addresses and telephone numbers duly exchanged with their newfound friends, it was back to their pond for another round of club sailing. Richard said his goodbyes to the vamp, but unfortunately the blond was nowhere to be seen...

The following weekend, the new pretenders forced upon themselves a proper debriefing session. Were they serious about this competitive sailing lark? If they were, what did they need to do to improve rankings – well, actually to gain a ranking? Was there any hope of them winning the odd trophy? These were big questions. But the answers – and they did eventually emerge – were harder to swallow.

They weren't good enough and by a long way. They needed new tonnage. Between them they had had a semblance of a budget but minimal knowledge of how to expand it. They needed to raise cash. And, even if they did, what on earth would they buy and equally, where could suitable sailboats be located?

'We could always ask yer man Dave for advice,' suggested Jonny. 'I mean, he's one of the leading lights isn't he?'

'Suppose,' said Richard.

Chapter Four

Beginning of the Beginning

Richard had to endure Jonny's blow-by-blow account of his Penny moments for a solid hour as they raced around the local club course, a conversational sail during which Jonny raised something his new girl friend had mentioned. It was a sailboat training session. Not exactly on their doorstep, but, said Jonny, an early start would get them there in time to participate. The highlight and key attraction, he went on, was that it would feature one of the country's leading yachtsmen doing the teaching.

'We really should go, Rich,' said Jonny, 'might even learn something.'

Being that bit older, and naturally wiser, Richard had immediate misgivings. By his club's standards this place would be way out of their league – for the wealthy only. They certainly were not wealthy. He was a lowly junior buyer and Jonny was a cash-strapped student and part-time bartender. Anyway, as far as Richard was concerned they would be a bunch of Hooray Henrys and snobs. They would certainly frown, he said, on the likes of us dropping in on their parade. Jonny, however, would not be dissuaded; he was smitten by Penny, and she had sold him the vision. He was still promoting the notion when they came ashore. Making little impact on his skipper, he tried another tangent. To Richard this seemed a bit underhanded.

'Look mate, you've got two choices as I see it,' Jonny said seriously.

Richard managed to sound dismissive and interested at the same time.

'Oh yeah?'

'It's like this.' He lowered his tone and his posture suggested the seriousness of the upcoming statement. Richard had planted his backside on the side-deck of another parked dinghy. His body had assumed a submissive but expectant slouch. He was ready.

'You – yes *you* Mr D'Arcy – introduced me to this game. You gave me an appetite for it and you also told me that you were the dog's bollocks – your words, not mine. Remember?' Richard nodded, fascinated but a little embarrassed, his arms tightly folded. He was wondering where this was all going.

'So, OK, we are shit hot on our wee pond – big fish. Give me a break Richard! If this is all there is, mate, then you know something? I'm better off behind a pair of oars.' Richard was on his feet now, treading the grass uneasily. He had misjudged this one – Jonny, he realised, was being deadly serious.

Is he really threatening to walk if I don't compromise on this?

Then Jonny threw him a lifeline.

'Oh, and by the way, it will be a mixed session. That means girls, Richard; you know — some of Penny's tribe... Might even be a friend in there for a wee home lovin' northern lad like you.'

Silence.

'Girls...' said Richard finally. 'Why didn't you say so?'

Richard grasped Jonny's ultimatum with a new sense of enthusiasm. 'That puts a whole new perspective on our sailing, Jonny boy. Tell me again. What time do we need to be ... Actually, at what unearthly hour would we need to leave?'

Jonny smiled.

Over the following weeks, Jonny and Richard kept returning to the subject of the training session. Richard continued to back-peddle, airing his misgivings. Finally it was narrowed down to two specific issues: first, he had conducted his own research and, as far as he could see, this training day was, in reality, no more than an old boys' get-together; a party, with teaching for cabaret. It was for their members and *their* guests. Secondly, even if they did decide to gate-crash, he really didn't want to show his pathetic little dinghy in public again. Julian's earlier description still jarred.

If he was to be really truthful – and Jonny eventually got him to admit it – he wanted neither of them to make fools of themselves. Certainly not in front of a bunch of trophied Hoorays.

They had bumped into Dave Gilmore sometime prior to the event. Over a few evening pints they talked it through. Dave knew the venue well. He knew some of the people who would be taking part – it was Julian's club. He did, however, agree that it was indeed a pretty upmarket set-up. His reassurances that the folk involved were 'good guys' did finally defrost Richard's attitude ... a little. Dave also confirmed that the training day would be no 'party', as Richard had christened it; with some frostiness he declared that the participants were serious and talented racers. Richard was privately unsure whether this was a good, or indeed an even worse, scenario. Me and my big mouth, he thought, but said nothing.

What an ace guy Dave turned out to be. Without a prompt he offered them the use of *his* boat. He also offered to deliver and rig it for them. After some persuasion they accepted his kind – barmy, they both thought – offer.

'No problem, Dave mate, thanks a million!' Accepting his terms and conditions, they looked at each other in disbelief.

'Jeez,' whispered Jonny. 'That boat's like a piece of furniture, Rich. What if we hit something? Or get hit? Or scratch it...?'

'We don't, and we won't,' was the somewhat terse reply from the skipper.

It was indeed like a piece of furniture. Constructed in marine ply, the boat was varnished inside and out. It actually glistened, even on a dull day, so rich was the gloss. Its overall appearance was that of mahogany; stately and strong. Its shape and sheer-line was emphasised by the white ash gunwale. A couple of inches below this, a gold pinstripe ran from bow to stern, a final touch that they agreed placed this craft in the limousine class.

This was a vessel that could grace the classiest showroom. In many ways it set the standard. It was a level to which all the other owners should aspire. Dave was, after all, national champion, and his was the top boat – she had style as well as performance.

It wasn't so much that Richard had been converted, it was more that he had been cleverly railroaded. He found himself at the point of no return. For some reason he was minded of the line: You can't push your way out through a door marked 'pull'. There was no way out, and the boat offer acted merely as the padlock. Whilst he remained outwardly anxious and sceptical, privately he was excited; he had an undying thirst for knowledge.

Chapter Five

First Impressions

It had been a seriously early start. Breakfast had been consumed by the roadside; greasy but edible. They had finally arrived feeling somewhat saddle sore. As they drew nearer their destination a silent aura of apprehension fell upon them. What lay ahead? The silence was very much of the 'real men don't wear pink' variety. Neither would, or could, voice their worries. It had been a quiet morning's drive, until they turned in through the imposing stone pillars of the club entrance. A brass plate glinted.

'Wow,' they uttered in unison, looking at each other. Some first impression! It also had the immediate effect of a tension button being released. Their first hurdle was cleared.

As they crept forward over the neatly marked out tarmac in search of suitable parking for Richard's little old frogeye Sprite, their twin 'petrol heads' clicked into gear. The automotive display that confronted them was, to say the least, striking. They immediately began ticking off noteworthy machinery. First: a couple of MGBs, one red, the other British Racing Green. They had been parked either side of a Sunbeam Rapier. She was pale blue with white flashed fins. Their car slowed to a crawl.

A drool over an immaculate yellow Triumph Stag followed – Richard had always dreamed of owning one – but as they rounded left towards the top row it was Jonny who took the lead in the over-excited category.

'Richard, Rich!' Jonny was standing up, leaning on the Sprite's windscreen frame and pointing. 'Look, it's a Rolls – a Silver Shadow.'

'Flippin''eck mate, so it is!' said Richard. They were like boys in a toy shop. Their concentration was now directed solely towards this aristocrat of motors. As their interest increased the engine revs decreased.

The Sprite came to an abrupt halt – stalled. Unabashed, both of them hopped out and bounded over to the Rolls for a closer look at the bodywork. They prodded the grill, stroked the panels, and of course caressed the *Spirit of Ecstasy*. Suddenly, both of them realised that they were actually standing there, exploring her curvaceous figure in full daylight. Chastened, they silently returned to the Sprite.

Further along there was a space between a red E-Type and a Rover 2000 TC. Reversing between them, Richard knew that he was thinking for both of them – are we indeed, he wondered, a bit out of our class? They were conducting a confirmation survey when their collective radar picked up another approaching vision, reminiscent of a mobile kaleidoscope... Strolling manfully across the car park, between an immaculate white MGA and a red round-tail Alpha Spyder, was the very striking figure of Julian.

He was resplendent in green tartan trousers held up with a broad white belt – above which, a purple flower-emblazoned shirt. His sartorial signature was completed by a plain dark, loosely knotted tie on which a small aircraft could have landed. It occurred to Richard that he clashed somewhat with the motors...

'Hello, you chaps. Thanks a bunch for coming along, come and meet the gang. Hey, cool car by the way.' They could see he meant it.

'Okay Jonny Boy,' said Richard quietly. 'Deep breath, there's no going back now.' He punched Jonny's shoulder. They didn't open the doors of the Sprite, just vaulted over. At that, Julian stopped Richard, pointed to a white notice plate peering down from above the Sprite's rear end.

'Ricky, old boy,' he said casually, 'nice bit of dismounting, but maybe you're not just in the best space, eh?' The penny dropped; he'd managed to plant his car in the space reserved for the club president.

'Suggest you chuck it over there beside that maroon Austin Cambridge.'

Richard grimaced privately. He hated being called Ricky. He re-parked as instructed. On closer inspection he noted that several spaces seemed to have been designated in the nautical: 'Commodore', 'Vice Commodore', 'Rear Commodore' and so on.

What sort of place, he wondered, were they getting themselves into? Privately his inner doubts were building into major reservations. Too late to back out now, he told himself. Julian breezed them past another row of exquisite motors, but just to bring Richard back to earth, a dented, brown Morris Marina tarnished the otherwise perfect scene.

A gently descending paved pathway led them past a rocky outcrop towards the clubhouse. It had an impressive Victorian facade in red brick, with a white-rendered second storey. To its left a slipway created a border between the manicured emerald lawn and a large hard area on which several sizeable and stately yachts stood propped, yet to be launched. Beside the grass a small dinghy park had been created. It had its own slipway; wide and concreted. It seemed that no expense had been spared here.

Richard was looking out for Dave's boat – their boat for the day – when an even more striking sight caught his attention. Dangling out from above a yellow hull, two beautiful, long, tanned legs disappeared into white shorts, exposing a narrow trace of red underwear.

'Eagle eyes or what?' He nudged Jonny.

'Clientele; Penny wasn't telling porkpies after all.' To Jonny, Richard was stating the obvious.

One by one, the attentive Julian introduced them to the gathering. Politely, hands were shaken and small talk dispensed. Julian insisted on introducing Richard as 'Ricky'.

'Richard D'Arcy,' Richard re-introduced himself, with an air of assertiveness. This caused Jonny to glance across, smirking. Penny, radiant in a denim miniskirt and a generously gaped white blouse, had briefly joined Jonny, but after placing a soft peck on his cheek she evaporated. Richard and Jonny momentarily felt alone; vulnerable, even. It felt like an age, but normal service was quickly resumed

Richard had dressed down, in jeans and black T-shirt. He continued to keep his counsel. In fact he had eased himself to the back of the circle – not at all like him. Jonny, on the other hand, distinctive in a red Fred Perry polo, took up centre court. The group now totalled twenty people – or nine crews' worth; two people per boat and one instructor, plus the driver of the club's 16-foot, navy blue launch.

Julian, his bleached blond spikes of hair oscillating in the late morning breeze, called the group to attention. He introduced the main man, the coach for the day, David Robinson. Richard stood to attention: *Flippin 'eck*, he thought *.He* is *a top man. Haven't I read him in the magazines? Yes, of course, he's the Olympic coach*! A now very attentive Richard, slightly flushed, realised for the first time that perhaps this day could offer just a little bit more than a tea party and a day's upper-class cruising. His insecurities were bubbling to the surface. His earlier assertiveness deserted him as he moved erratically from foot to foot, hands shoved deep into pockets. He reverted to wondering: was he, were *they*, good enough for this line-up? At this stage, if an exit had appeared, he might easily have disappeared back to his cabbage patch of a club, where he was king. His nerves had momentarily got the better of him. Perhaps, he thought, there is merit in being a small town big-timer. He tried to convince himself as he searched for that exit route...

'OK skipper, ready to rock'n'roll?' Jonny's voice yanked him back to reality.

As a closet architecture enthusiast, Richard's eyes were bouncing from feature to imposing feature of this magnificent structure as they all made their way into, and through the clubhouse to the briefing room. The distraction was more than enough to settle him, almost too much...

If the spectacle of the clubhouse facade was not enough, the decorative architrave, plasterwork and general decor now demanded his attention. The oak panelling, bestowed with gilt-framed portraits of commodores past, and various grand yachting scenes of a bygone era, completed the set for Richard. He could easily have spent the morning ashore, absorbing the grandeur. But there was a spot of training to be getting on with. Although softening to the surroundings, Richard remained reluctant to release the final strings of reality. In an attempt to find a semblance of equilibrium, he babbled to himself.

'Hardly the Long Lake.' Then he wondered, 'Is this how the Royal Yacht Squadron at Cowes is decked out behind that frontage of starting cannons and yardarms?' His protective shield had perhaps not melted, but its surface had certainly softened.

As the briefing outlined the day's schedule of events, the group – even Richard – mingled. The boys had found themselves, perhaps not quite the centre of attention, but certainly made to feel most welcome by this eclectic group of people. It was a strange environment for them. Whilst the expected snobbery did not materialise, the politeness with which they were greeted was perhaps a little forced. Nevertheless, it was welcome. For the moment, they maintained a discreet distance.

As they filed into their respective changing rooms Julian took the opportunity to make a personal introduction. Richard met Samantha. She had missed the initial introductions. 'Sam, meet Ricky,' said Julian.

'Richard, actually.' As he shook hands, it dawned on him that she was the legs hanging out of the boat.

He was immediately fixated, tantalised, felt he knew her already. Standing equal in height, he was paralysed by her natural beauty. Blond hair combed back from a high forehead; sweeping eyebrows emphasising radiant green eyes. Her poise – her presence – rendered him dumb-struck to the point of concussion. It was as if he had entered the eye of a sensualised hurricane – the two of them locked in an instant connection. The outside world seemed to spin around them. He remained oblivious in the privacy of their sanctum. Reluctant to let the moment go, he steadied himself – what could he say?

'So — the legs do go the whole way up...'

Oh shit. I've done it again. Made a complete ass of myself – why can't I just be normal, just for once? He was stunned and appalled by his wisecracking indiscretion.

'I'm sorry, I meant…'

But it was too late. She didn't even smile. She freed her hand, turned, and walked away. The spell broken – blown – and he was unceremoniously catapulted back to reality. Even Julian must have felt the shockwave: he too had walked away.

Richard quickly refocused his attentions. He needed something, anything, to grasp onto; alternatively, a hole to disappear down …

Careful not to catch anyone's eye, he wandered aimlessly off, and found himself entering the blessed refuge of the male changing area. The entire home clubhouse, he decided, would fit inside this room. The Long Lake changing facility was basically a garden shed attached to the rear of the main building. It was nothing more than a little annex, a bare room, concrete floor with two toilet cubicles and a single washbasin moulded into one corner.

On a warm, wet afternoon it could get quite steamy, and pungent. This place – well, how the other half lived ...

But is it homely? he mused sarcastically. Trying hard to banish his faux pas, he studied and mused in silence, continuing his absurd little survey.

Tiled floors, personalised lockers, a separate shower area – it's got one, two, three…six shower heads and a suite of toilets. A chap could get used to this.

'How much, to be a member here?' he said aloud.

'Sorry old boy, what did you say?' A figure appeared from round a corner, halfway into his wet suit.

'Oh, err, nothing mate; just thinking aloud.'

Perhaps I'll enquire when I'm head buyer; but then again, perhaps not...

His conversation with himself had concluded.

He bumped into Samantha again as the group, now clad in sailing attire, exited the building. If anything, she looked even better in neoprene. He apologised, and she managed a smile. Richard nodded, relieved, but he said no more. *Richard*, he thought, *be*

careful, son. This girl is way out of your league. Besides, she's
bound to be hooked up with one of these Hoorays…

As he made his way towards the dinghy enclosure, one thought, in spite of everything, kept recurring. Had he imagined it, or was there something about the way *she* looked at *him*?

Half an hour later, Dave's boat was finally fully rigged; they were afloat, the last crew to leave the slipway.

Jonny and Richard agreed that it had been an excellent day out. It had been like a lifting fog; a mountain of information amassed. Their haul was not only from David Robinson, the coach, but from several within the group. They swallowed hard on humble pie. The group, and even the non-participating members of this Royal club, had been overwhelmingly welcoming, polite and helpful.

Showered and prettied, they rejoined the group within the quaintness of the members' downstairs bar. But they had donned their sensible heads. They aimed to quit while they were ahead.

En masse, the group headed for the clubhouse restaurant. Expressing their thanks amidst a flurry of waving hands and cheerio's, they excused themselves. But not before Richard, ever the trier, said his personal cheerio to the lovely Samantha.

She was even more stunning than before, in a flowing full-length off-the-shoulder summer dress of green and red. Her hair was still wet. She was indeed beautiful. Goodbyes said, they finally headed for the door, along the Italian-tiled corridor. Samantha unexpectedly re-emerged from the restaurant side door. Gliding towards them, she seemed to be heading for Richard. She stopped a few feet from him and asked, somewhat assertively, her voice now low and toned, more polite than posh:

'Richard, umm, maybe we'll catch up again – at the next event?'

The result of this turn of events was that he missed the step at the front door. His exit provided the audience on the lawn with a hilarious performance of the Rubber Band Man – he landed pretty awkwardly but his jack-in-the-box return to the vertical was, he felt, impressive.

'I'm OK, no problem,' he said, taking Samantha's outstretched hand and hobbling back into the porch. His exit had been nothing if not dramatic. Samantha managed to keep a straight face – Jonny, less so. Glancing sternly at Jonny, Samantha showed a clear concern for Richard's well-being. Somewhat pale in the cheeks, he again reassured all present.

'Honestly, I'm OK, no harm done.'

He found himself looking directly into Samantha's eyes, and tried to carry on where they'd left off.

'Yeah, yeah. Brill. Absolutely, yes. I'll look forward to that. Wow!'

Still somewhat flustered, an elated Richard was oblivious to the pain. Chuckling, Samantha had turned to rejoin her friends. Her hand now covered her generous lips. She was a little flushed. As she disappeared through the oak doors of the restaurant, she again

gestured acceptance of their 'date' with a nod, and a little wave.
Richard, as usual, was way ahead of himself. I should, he thought,
have reached over and kissed her – on the cheek, of course. Ah well.

And with that, the boys were also gone, headed for the car park.
Out of sight, the pain finally exploded. Leaning heavily on Jonny,
Richard, whose pallor was now fully translucent, limped all the way
back up to the car. His ankle was inflating like a balloon. He
couldn't drive, and the journey would be agony – the Sprite was
never famed for its suspension.

Richard never got to inspect those beautiful yachts, the finer
details of the building – or indeed the owner of the Silver Shadow.

'Hey Ricky, Mr Robinson gave me his business card. Cool, eh?'
Jonny was excited as he fired up the frog-eye. Richard, fighting the
pain, replied somewhat disinterestedly.

'Teacher's pet. And by the way, the name's Richard.'

'Okay okay, little man, don't take your love life out on me. And
by the way, you can also take those marbles out of your mouth. It's
me you're sitting beside, not that posh bird in the porch.'

He looked at his skipper.

'Do you really, really think you've got a chance there mate?' He
shook his head. 'You've no chance. She's way out of your league.'

It was a very grumpy Richard who felt, and endured, every
bump on the road home that memorable day. Each and every
undulation, cat's eye or pebble telegraphed a pulse of pain through

to his ankle. The aspirins his mate produced, three of them, made little difference.

'Jeez mate, you don't look too great,' said Jonny with a wry smile. 'Crikey, I've seen better looking corpses...'

Richard didn't rise, and Jonny continued to warble on about the sailing. Richard's mind was drifting: finance, pain, drowsiness, the exquisite Samantha. Posh bird or not, he just knew that they had bonded; there had been a spark. He was already planning their next encounter. Turning to Jonny, he declared suddenly:

'We'll see. Just you watch this space, Jonny boy.'

Richard had thrown down the gauntlet.

Chapter Six

New Tonnage

By the following weekend Richard was mobile. More to the point as
far as he was concerned, they were able to meet up with Dave
Gilmore again. The venue was an aged country pub on the outskirts
of Chester. It had just gone 11:30 a.m. Expressing their sincere and
collective thanks – with a bottle – they provided him with a
verbatim report.

Little did they know that Dave was an old friend of David
Robinson – he was well aware of their classroom performance.
Behind the scenes it was Dave who had facilitated the day. The big
issue, Richard had told him in an earlier telephone conversation, a
day or so after their day out, that sailing his boat had underpinned,

once and for all, that they had outlived their existing craft. Richard had confirmed to Dave that evening of their need for new tonnage.

In terms of finance, Richard had a few pounds in a savings account, as had Jonny. After a modicum of family 'sponsorships' and, as it turned out, a supportive bank manager, they had accumulated their budget. A budget that, Richard reckoned, would comfortably stretch to the right boat.

Dave was an interesting character, his rough-neck, tattooed appearance belying a soft and caring nature. Heavily built, he stood at some 5'8". A thick, short neck seemed to mould itself seamlessly into a facial symmetry, which featured a deep-set pair of doleful eyes. His slightly kiltered nose was unmistakeable, almost distracting. He was a caricature, the kind of figure you expect to find on a nightclub doorway. Indeed his appearance, in a sense, was unfortunate, because a more gentle, supportive and humorous man you could not expect to meet. The time and effort he had devoted to their predicament was testament. Even before they had settled into a window alcove and before Richard got in the first round of drinks, it was clear that Dave was way ahead of them. He produced a list of five buyable boats, all of which he deemed good value. Then systematically he went through each craft in detail, explaining the various pros, cons and, of course, pedigree – the all-important race-winning potential.

Noon passed, their debating lubricated by the occasional 'small sherry'. Finally and unanimously they agreed that boat number three, in spite of her name, was to be their prime target. At that, Dave extracted himself. He moved with purpose in the general direction of the toilets, dredging a handful of coins from his pocket. His exit gave the boys, reeling in the turbulence of his considerable wake, time to consider their position.

It also provided Richard with the opportunity to run his eye over the inside of this old building. In some ways it was not unlike The Cellars. It was softer in décor, though, and more symmetrical in layout. Under a low-beamed ceiling a circular bar reached out into the main lounge area. To its right was the corridor, down which Dave had disappeared. He supposed it led off to toilets, a darts room or perhaps a snug. On the opposite side, he noticed glazed doors, leading into what appeared to be a pretty posh restaurant. Several of the tables within the bar area were set up for lunch. Cutlery wrapped in red tissue. An early clientele was filing in. The carvery was giving off a tempting aroma, which suggested to Richard that a bite of lunch would not go amiss...

'Hello...Earth to Richard...hello...' Jonny attempted to reel his buddy back in.

'Oh. Sorry mate – just admiring the surroundings. You should bring Penny here. She'd love you for it. I'm starving, how about you?'

'More important issues to consider, skipper.'

Dave duly returned carrying another round of drinks: Carling Black Label for Johnny, Coke Cola for Richard and another whiskey for himself. Passing round the drinks, he revealed that he had telephoned the owner of the selected craft and confirmed their interest.

'Flippin 'eck Dave, you don't hang about, do you?' said Richard, now fully back in the conversation.

Dave's reaction was immediate and terse. Still standing, he affected his most menacing, no-nonsense persona.

'Listen boys,' he said. 'If you want to win races you can't continue to sit on your arse, and fart around. That boat won't sit for long. Tomorrow morning suit you for a viewing?'

He reunited himself with the booth.

Richard looked at Jonny, who nodded.

'Em, err, yeah, yeah, good for us – what time?' said Richard.

'10 a.m. sharp,' was the reply. Then Dave threw back the remains of his whiskey and stood up.

'Just one thing, Dave,' enquired Jonny. 'Where exactly are we going?'

Dave extracted a black biro from the sleeve pocket of his anorak, and jotted down the address on the back of a Guinness beer mat. Then he was gone.

A somewhat shell-shocked duo were boyishly excited at the prospect of having a new toy, and for an hour, between forkfuls of hot-pot, they spoke of little else. They talked over one another, sketching plans on the paper napkins, conferring. By mid-afternoon they had finally exhausted their day of nauticalia. Strolling towards the toilets in preparation for the homeward jaunt the conversation again turned back to Dave. Now standing side by side at the urinals it was Jonny who filled in the obvious gap in their observations of this new found friend and benefactor...

'Bloody hell, Rich, that boy sure likes his drink.'

'From a cola perspective, that's an understatement,' said Richard. They both agreed, but thought no more of it.

'Thank goodness you're driving, mate; too much lager.' concluded Jonny but not before he had expelled a rattling burst of wind. They were the only occupants.

By noon the following day they were the proud new owners of *Kittiwake.* She was 15ftlong, painted orange and barely two years old; a proper racing dinghy. The package, thought Richard, represented terrific value. It included not only a brand new road trailer but a green canvas all-weather cover and a brand new unused suit of sails. There were also a number of accessories, and multiples of other used sails of varying quality.

She sported a beautifully varnished wooden deck of veneered sapele plywood. It radiated richness in the mid-morning sunlight. The boat's layout featured an array of modern fittings in stainless steel and black plastic. It all came in at well under what they had considered would be the going rate. Not a bad morning's work, they agreed.

Richard ran his hand across her deck. It was like a piece of furniture; a hall table. They now owned what his father would call a *real* boat, fit to race. Jonny was particularly excited. This was a whole new experience for him. His thoughts turned to that infamous regatta. Now he was the co-owner of a boat that was the equal of any of those they had drooled over. He had borrowed his dad's silver Volvo, which had a tow-bar; Jonny had naturally assumed that a sale would be agreed.

True to form, Dave was there when they arrived, talking boats with the owner.

Introductions made and a deal was duly done, A deal done on Richard's terms; even outside working hours he found himself unable to ditch his buyer's instinct. Jonny nervously attempted to hitch the trailer onto the car's tow-bar. Dave, obviously frustrated by Jonny's faffing, intervened and completed the hitching process.

'You can't afford to be timid with tow-hitches Jonny boy,' he said. 'Got to make sure they are securely clicked together and shipshape, yes?' Dave had slipped back into lecture mode. 'Don't want to be picking your lovely lady out of a ditch on the way to her new home, eh?'

He proceeded to unhitch the rig and made Jonny complete the whole exercise again. He also demonstrated various other procedures, the principle one being how best to secure a boat to a road trailer. Meanwhile, and away from the trailer action, Richard's habitual curiosity – nosiness, if he was honest – had led him back into conversation with the vendor.

Midway in, he wished he hadn't.

The real reason that *Kittiwake* was on the market at, what Dave considered to be, a knockdown price, a steal even, very quickly became evident. Barkley Brown was a middle-ranking industrial chemist who had, some nine months earlier, been sacked over some sort of internal misdemeanour. He had so far failed to find re-employment. With bills piling up, the mortgage people chasing him and, he confided, his marriage in turmoil, he was being forced to liquidate his key assets. But when Richard was in buyer's mode, he felt no guilt.

An hour had passed, and Jonny was not terribly amused. Dave, streetwise as ever, had quietly extracted himself before Richard asked his fateful question.

Finally on the road, the first comment was not from Jonny.

'Yes, yes, I know – don't start on me,' appealed Richard. There followed an embarrassing pause.

'Don't fancy the colour much,' said Jonny, breaking the silence. Richard had to agree.

The drive back to their club was not so much slow, as careful. They were anxious to show off their prize in one piece, and in any case Richard's first job, when they arrived, would be to post a 'For Sale' sign against his existing boat.

'*Kittiwake!*' said Jonny. 'Jeez Rich, we can't go racing with name like that.' Richard agreed, and for the next hour and a half's drive-time they debated. Song title after song title, among other submissions, was presented for suitability, then rejected. In the end they had eliminated 'Tumblin Dice', 'Canned (& in) Heat' and 'The Last Time', in favour of 'Satisfaction'– it was always going to be a Rolling Stones title in spite of Jonny's infuriating habit of chucking in little known titles from his back knowledge of 'the blues' legends. Legends, such as Leadbelly, T-bone Walker, Hooker and so on... Richard generally switched off when his mate went into condescending student speak. The detail of the new livery could wait for another day. Their main priority was to hear the crackle of pristine sailcloth, and experience again the liveliness of a new and lighter vessel, under their backsides.

Arriving at the Long Lake by mid-afternoon, they parked beside the old boat in the club dinghy enclosure. Although they were of the same design, the two boats were as different as night and day. Richard and Jonny agreed that to have achieved what they did in the 'old girl' had taken her way past her capabilities. So, well done us! Self-congratulation, however, was tempered by the realisation that the acquisition of *Kittiwake,* now re-named *Satisfaction,* had exhausted the boys' current cargo of excuses.

It was the third day of March. If their new mistress was to be readied in time for the myriad of events in the upcoming regatta season – and the challenges they would bring – they had better complete this colour change and get practicing!

Chapter Seven

Glossing Up

The university had broken up for Easter. Jonny offered to do the toiling on the boat, which essentially meant rubbing back the existing orange paint on the hull to prepare a keying surface for new paintwork. Richard was unavoidably busy at work: sheaf's of tender documents required posting out to potential suppliers before the holiday closure. The overtime was great for the money, but ate up precious evenings and weekends.

In a week Jonny, ably assisted by the lovely Penny and, of course, 'supervised' by Richard's dad, had made significant progress. Not only was the paintwork flattened and faired but father D'Arcy had applied a grey undercoat. The hull sat readied for the first of at least four layers of gloss, if ever they all could agree on a colour.

It was now Saturday. The sun was shafting through the high windows of the big brick garage at the rear of the D'Arcy's' suburban semi. They gazed on their upturned lady. No further progress had been achieved on the colour. Work had ground to a standstill. Penny, breaking the deadlock, proposed that the obvious colour was staring straight back at them.

'Grey.'

To which the assembled gathering reacted in unison.

'GREY?'

'Look,' she explained in an assertive, art teacher sort of way, 'you've got a big bright purple and orange spinnaker so you need a neutral-coloured hull to emphasise it, not fight with it, understand?' The gathered males simultaneously dropped their heads, and there followed a funereal silence. Penny, however, was at art college. She knew things.

'...So grey it is then.' Richard broke the silence. 'Let's buy paint, grey paint.'

Penny drove. Jonny braced himself. Richard clutched the International Paints brochure. He was riding shotgun. He bounced around the backseat of the Mini. They were making good time. The nearest chandlery store was on the outskirts of nearby Stoke-on-Trent.

The boys, Jonny in particular, were still somewhat unconvinced by Penny's artistic direction. But at least they were in agreement. Well... no, they weren't. They had gone along with Penny's view because they hadn't come up with an alternative. Happy enough to play for extra time by browsing various shades of grey, they hoped that the 'right' colour would jump out at them. It didn't. Then, while studying various brand options, Richard recalled an article he had read in one of his many yachting magazines. It was written by a successful racer – he couldn't remember the name. The writer suggested that grey was in fact an excellent colour for starting line manoeuvres. He said that a boat, which was painted grey, was not easy to identify in a crowded fleet. Very much like a warship. The article, Richard recalled, went on to suggest that within a big fleet if you were a little premature at starting, as indeed they had a tendency to be, it could be the difference between a false and a great start.

'If it's good enough for the Navy...'

'Sorry, Rich? Navy...?' Penny threw her eyes to heaven. 'Well that's different, I'm sure – there won't be more than a dozen navy hulls in the boat park. Huh.'

'I meant *Royal* Navy... Oh, never mind; grey it is.'

After the best part of an hour's faffing, shuffling tins around and mumbling, Jonny was outvoted, 2:1. On the advice of the bemused counter staff, they opted for a Rylard enamel as opposed to the common brand: slightly more expensive, but Penny was assured that it would flow better and cure harder.

'Three tins please.' Richard had been nominated purser for the day. On the basis that if Penny was happy, he was happy, Jonny said nothing.

Approaching the mini, Jonny offered Richard the front seat. But the offer was quietly refused, both agreeing that Penny had obviously been a pupil at the Paddy Hopkirk School of Driving. Although she was by no means a fast driver, she nevertheless had a habit of maintaining a constant speed – on the straight, and round the bends. On the occasions when she did change gear, the clutch was never over used. The road-holding capability of the Mini was impressive, if not the bum-holding capability of the rear seats …

For Richard, meeting up with Penny again had brought good vibrations. Warm memories of that training session she had helped to engineer came to the surface. It of course aroused charged thoughts and romantic visions of the upmarket Samantha. Indeed Sam, whilst obviously out of his league, had rarely been out of his thoughts. Wholly smitten, he was already fantasising about their next encounter, their first date.

Whilst her image had been well and truly imprinted on his consciousness, typical of Richard he still knew absolutely nothing about her – he had never even bothered to identify the guy who had been her skipper for that day. Thinking it through, he reckoned he must have been her boy friend. So, in truth, a fantasy was all that he had. But then again, he told himself, it was actually she who had befriended him on that day. Logically speaking, it would be only a matter of time before *she* would make contact; after all, it was she who had made the first move.

This sudden rush of blood to the head only subsided when he recalled that during their fleeting encounter it was *he* who had performed like a babbling idiot.

What happened to me that day? Will I ever really see her again? Richard's thought processes were in overdrive. *Oh bugger, how do I get myself into these conundrums. Why aren't things simple and straightforward? Because I'm Richard bloody D'Arcy.*

Learning from Penny that Julian had taken up a short-term post in the United States, he finally concluded that all his avenues of exploration had been transformed into one romantic cul de sac. Remembering the gauntlet he had thrown down, he determined that she would be found. but he was reconciled to a fruitless encounter. He figured calmly that she was bound to appear on the regatta circuit. Certainly, he would have no problem recognising her again; she was, he thought, a dead ringer for Judy Geeson, blond bob and all. And with that he signed off. He had neatly consigned the Samantha search to his mental 'pending' file.

It was lunchtime at the D'Arcy household; just after 12:30. Chicken soup was on the menu, a speciality of Richard's mum Molly. The team needed sustenance for the next stage of the mistress's makeover. The final glossing of the good ship *Satisfaction* was just days away, her orange livery completely consigned to history.

By 4:30 p.m., the day's labours of love were completed. Having cleaned up, they retired to the front room of number 36. In glorious colour, the football results were studied. Richard, stretched out on the deep-pile Axminster carpet, checked off his pools. Coupon checked. He came to terms with the fact that it would be back to work as usual on Monday… Jonny had long since excused himself, having seen the 'Villa score.

Midweek, under a polythene tent he had carefully erected inside the garage to minimise dust particles, Richard's dad laid on the last layer of gloss. Jonny had earlier completed the final fairing session. The paint was allowed to fully cure – *Satisfaction* lay undisturbed for the remainder of the week.

Returning from the office that Friday evening, Richard's first port of call was of course the tent. The guy at the chandlery store was not spoofing – the finish achieved was testament. His tip about thinning down the final layer, his dad told him, was spot on – what a shine! Richard was ecstatic, and father D'Arcy, always a stickler, was well impressed too.

Jonny and his old man popped round, as did Dave, Michael Murphy and Richard's brother-in-law Iain. The finished product was touched and stroked and commented on. But to Richard's dad's utter horror it was suggested that they should 'flatten' the underside of the hull to a mat finish. This, Dave explained, was to improve the laminar flow of water over the hull. With some reluctance, Richard and Jonny agreed. Arthur D'Arcy, outvoted on this occasion, leant a hand, and the shine was quickly removed from the mistress's nether regions.

Then, with everybody helping, even the dads, she was efficiently turned upright, settled onto her bespoke trailer and readied for a Long Lake equivalent of the morning tide. With that, the party retired to the D'Arcy's front room, where there awaited one of Molly's classic celebration spreads. Jonny didn't stay too long, his date with Penny had prior call. Dr. Dubois, however, was harder to shift; he and Richard's dad had become lost in conversation and wine tasting.

Saturday dawned. It was, as the Scots would say, 'dreich'. Everything – the sky, the water, *Satisfaction's* hull and the Volvo – seemed to merge into one colour: grey, grey and more grey. An attempt to record events with the Super 8 Cine was abandoned, the lens misted. Conditions perfectly mirrored the internal state of a few heads, the previous evening's culinary spread having been washed down with a seemingly endless supply of Blue Nun and various brands of beer. A steady drizzle seemed to permeate everyone and everything.

At least the breeze was starting to ripple the surface of Long Lake. After three-quarters of an hour's fiddling, the good ship *Satisfaction* was finally rigged. Her crew, satisfied that everything was in its designated position, the pristine Bruce Banks Terylene sails now bent on and ready for hoisting, stood back to admire. Then Richard and Jonny retired to their bijou changing room while the dads retreated to the Volvo.

They remained afloat for the best part of two hours, oblivious to the freshening conditions, and returned to shore around 3:30 p.m. They were in jubilant form. Every penny that had so far been spent on the former *Kittiwake* was worth it. To cap the day off, the dads had had the foresight to take the boys' clothes home and dry them out. Within the sanctum of the changing room, skipper Richard signed off the day by quoting his father:

'Ay, young Jonny – a grand day out indeed.'

A somewhat bemused Jonny said nothing, just gave him one of his looks. Smiling thinly, he wondered, not for the first time, whether his skipper was actually beginning to turn into his father.

As a bonus, Richard even sold his own boat to another club member that very evening, thus reducing his general indebtedness. His dad wouldn't take any money, suggesting instead that he should replenish his savings account, or use it to open a joint 'boat account' at the bank.

Richard took his mum and dad out for Sunday lunch the next day at the local hotel. They appreciated that.

Chapter Eight

Upping the Stakes

The results from a series of early season regattas were promising. And by the completion of that first full season the D'Arcy-Dubois team was already ranking just outside the top ten. It was a satisfactory and positive return. They had looked long, listened hard and learned a lot. During those six hectic months their ability to digest how others handled themselves was textbook. They mimicked racing styles relentlessly, always practicing, always testing. The reward was a wave of onwards and upwards propulsion. Dave Gilmore, the reigning champion, was impressed; he made no secret of it. He had, in a real sense, mentored them, and the early fruits of his labour were extremely positive.

Because of their hunger for success, one difficult decision – for Richard certainly – required action. The subject was breached on several occasions but they kept postponing the obvious and inevitable.

They had outgrown the Long Lake. Every time they sailed there in club competitions they found themselves deliberately slowing their boat, resorting to being late afloat, racing with the sails over-taut, or even flapping. Sometimes they 'accidentally' got themselves positioned the wrong side of the starting line, thus allowing their competition a head start. Certainly it presented a challenge, made a race of it, but it added little to their overall performance targets. They became proficient at carving out a route from last to first, happy to concede that this particular skill might well come in useful some day. Overall, a lack of quality boat-to-boat duelling would make them vulnerable – an experienced competitor could easily exploit the weakness.

The writing was on the wall, and the last piece of their exit jigsaw fitted into place when they became convinced that *they* had become something of a deterrent at Long Lake. Their acquired status of being 'unbeatable' had, it seemed to them, contributed to a slump in the club's race-day turnouts.

'So much for success breeding success, skipper,' Jonny commented.

Approval was far from universal amongst club members, but they had to move, preferably to a club where the skill level was high and the racing ethos sound.

He talked it through with his dad – a founder member – who asked, to Richard's complete surprise, why they had taken so long. He confided that he had been waiting for this move, that he had his own decisions to make.

What Richard had thought was just a personal observation as to the demise of competitive sailing was, it seemed, not an entirely inaccurate assessment after all. There had indeed been a change in atmosphere at Long Lake. The cold shoulder treatment, and the snide remarks passed on to them over the off-season, merely acted to reinforce their decision but they were blind to what was emerging from behind the scenes.

Arthur D'Arcy didn't resign, but he stepped away from committee, telling Richard that the club is always bigger than the sum of the individual members. He maintained the link, just in case.

However, and against Arthur D'Arcy's advice, an extraordinary general meeting was called at the club. A motion to drop the word 'sailing' from the club's title was carried with a strong majority, and plans were laid to develop the lake for fishing. Sometime later it was sold off to a commercial leisure company. D'Arcy senior wasn't unduly concerned: unlike Richard, he enjoyed nothing more than a day's fishing...

Chapter Nine

Highs, Lows and Love Lost

Over the winter they tackled the ergonomics of their craft. More or less every fitting was either replaced or beefed-up and repositioned. This, alas, left its beautiful varnished deck a little 'spotty'. It was a major programme of works, but it was necessary to minimise gear failure – as it turned out, the season's nemesis.

Believing they were now good enough, Richard and Jonny had become, two seriously focused individuals. The national title was the goal. To have retired in three of the five races at their first attempt at the title was not particularly auspicious for a pair of budding superstars. Beauty therefore had to give way to staying power.

The season had been a real rollercoaster for Richard. The big high was winning their first race, ironically at that national series. The low was that he never did get to see the lovely Samantha again. He consoled himself with the belief that there had been a distinct spark – but conceded that it must have been all but extinguished. He never forgot his gauntlet though, and he didn't like to lose.

Jonny was far too polite to even raise the matter.

Late one evening, enjoying the quiet of an empty house, Richard was watching TV, slouched in an old armchair. Beer in one hand, crisps in the other, he caught the late film, *Three Into Two Won't Go*. He was fixated by the scene where Geeson, in tight white t-shirt and jeans, slid into the passenger seat of Rod Steiger's car and stretched out. Suddenly, Richard found himself transported back to those memorable moments of the training day; Judy Geeson was, in that moment, the lovely Samantha.

A few weeks later, and to his utter shame, he knowingly took his new and striking girlfriend of several weeks to see the horror film *Doomwatch*. Who shared the starring role?

Sarah, from the accounts department, just a little shorter than him, was a stylish nineteen-year-old brunette. Long silky hair fell over her shoulders to compliment a mannequin figure. At work her complexion, sans make-up, was fresh. Satin skin the pallor of buttermilk, nose petite and eyes a mysterious grey. Made up, she was sensational. His circle of male friends was envious. For the most part, they couldn't understand what she saw in him;

nevertheless, they were impressed. Jonny and Penny were stunned – but touchingly pleased, adding only that they hoped he wouldn't screw it all up with his habit of treating his girlfriends to ill-thought-out wise cracks.

It was during a break in proceedings at a charity event hosted by the local netball team – she played wing attack – that they connected. She was selling raffle tickets, he was in the throes of apologising for an earlier spat in the office over late payments, when their unlikely liaison gelled.

The consensus among his friends was that, by assuming more responsibility at work, a maturity had rooted within young D'Arcy. There was a newfound confidence about him, fuelled by those successes afloat. Of course a rising financial status, augmented by his music management sideline, provided him with an expanded portfolio of social opportunities. His horizons had widened; hence, perhaps, the developing relationship with Sarah.

Watching the film, and Geeson in particular, Richard felt a pang of guilt. He felt like a two-timer; a man with a girl on both arms. His left arm was draped around Sarah's shoulder, and his right around a virtual Samantha. Anyway, whether it was because they saw too much of each other too soon, or his guilt began to intrude, their early passion gradually cooled. The relationship foundered. It was an amicable split in the end. Both agreed that it was going nowhere. However, they remained friends, and in due course he was even invited to her wedding.

Sarah remained arguably, the most beautiful girl he had ever dated. On reflection, and considering the incident of the 'flicks', the relationship, fated though it was, was good for Richard. It had provided him with a glimpse of a settled state; perhaps it helped him reappraise his thinking on romance. No more one-nightstands, well, if possible.

He knew that if Jonny ever got to know about that night he would never let him forget it. He resolved to say nothing, and grow up. Beyond the odd weekend, Richard didn't see much of Jonny over the winter. His dentistry career was entering a more serious chapter, as was his relationship with Penny; but the two friends remained in telephone contact even though their social brotherhood was beginning to drift. Jonny and Penny had very much moved to the cultural while Richard remained 'one of the lads'.

Maintenance became the norm for Sunday mornings at Ashley Road. On one occasion, Richard was crouched, twisted uncomfortably beneath the side-deck, holding a small spanner which was in turn locked onto a stainless steel nut. Body and head seemed disconnected; only his plumber's bum and splayed legs were visible. Jonny, his usual cool self, was positioned on the outside of the boat ready for the instruction to turn the bolt with a screwdriver.

Jonny said casually: 'Rich, you know that bird you keep warbling on about?'

'What *do* you mean, Mr Dubois?' came the muffled reply.

'Well, I was meandering down a hospital corridor last week and bumped into her; actually, it was she who recognised me – couldn't blame her for that of course.'

'WHAT! Ow fuck!!' The spanner had slipped – yet another skinned knuckle – and he cracked the side of his head as he extricated himself. More expletives. Richard could not believe what he was hearing.

'Well?!' he demanded.

'Yeah –' Jonny continued to relay the detail of the encounter, but in an economical fashion. 'She was asking about you. And, she appeared to know lots about our exploits.' He was calm – the exact opposite of Richard's precipitated state. Jonny good-naturedly continued his news bulletin, but there was a mischievous undertone in his delivery. He explained that whilst *she* was unable to get much sailing in due to some family issues, she was keeping up with their progress through the yachting press.

'*Yachting & Boating Weekly* and *Yachts and Yachting* her main source.'

With that, Jonny concluded his report.

'Unfortunately that's all the information I have for you, mate. I got called away and we never did meet up again; sor-ry.' Jonny, palms outstretched, shrugged his shoulders and quickly changed tack. He upped his vocals in both tone and pace.

'So, what do think of that, Ricky boy. We're national news, eh?'

Richard remained lost in thought, his eyes dancing. Jonny continued to talk – but he knew only too well what to expect. He was attempting to outrun Richard, but another eruption was expected any second. He chatted on, mentally counting down: *four, three, two.....*

'... And I thought we were just local news, no wider that the Chronicle.' He was down to small talk now, cringing and clinching. He had hardly finished the word 'chronicle' when it blew – and that, he knew, was the end of the morning's work schedule.

The probing that followed laid waste upon Jonny; it was more an inquisition than a conversation. Samantha, it seemed, was a nurse, but not at Jonny's Birmingham hospital – she was merely there on a course when the encounter happened.

'What kind of bloody help is that?' Richard slammed the spanner down, denting the deck, wiped his hands across the back-side of his black jeans and stormed out into the late morning sun to cool down. En route, tripping over an open toolbox, he made a final, fatal remark over his shoulder:

'Thanks a flamin bunch mate – thanks for nothing!'

Jonny looked defensive, unsure; even he seemed taken aback at his mate's outburst of aggression – wondering, perhaps, whether he should even have mentioned the encounter at all. But in the ensuing silence his demeanour changed. He turned and glared at Richard. Taking a deep breath he carefully set his screwdriver down. With a 'tut' he stroked his fore finger over the dented deck. Quietly but with obvious intent he followed Richard into the garden. Beside the greenhouse he paused. His stare was now locked on Richard, and with pointed finger he opened his retaliation.

'YOU! Oh, how the mighty are fallen. And after the shit I had to take when me and Penny firmed up.'

Jonny had closed in on Richard's space, but now he took a step back.

'Ricky mate, the difference here is that I'm not chasing a bloody shadow... So do yourself a big favour, and grow up!' There followed an uneasy silence. Richard noticed his parents peeping out from the kitchen window. At one stage he had thought he was going to get punched.

Realising what an idiot he had been, Richard quickly apologised.

In an instant they returned to their normal banter, and Jonny actually volunteered to track Samantha down; to try to fill in at least some more of the blanks, dissipate the shadows. Mercifully, there was work to be done – even more important, they agreed, than Richard's elusive love life. The mistress would have her two admirers to herself again, for at least the rest of the day. It was approaching noon; Richard's sartorial profile was now grease stained but his mate's had remained virgin white.

Chapter Ten

Changed Times Indeed

Richard and Jonny met up with their new club mates in late August. They competed in the final series of the club's season. Two races were held every Saturday. Fourteen boats were lined across the starting line for the first race. Unlike the Long Lake there were open expanses of deep water which produced significant waves; different and difficult conditions for them to master. But there was real competition, especially when the wind blew. At some 1,000 feet above sea level it always seemed to blow! This was a new beginning and no quarter was given or expected.

Although they hoped for better, the new boys didn't exactly cover themselves in glory on their first outing. But they agreed that it had been a learning curve. Of course, their new chums were not

72

expected to be walkovers. After all, among this fleet were a number of championship-level sailors. Changed times? Changed times indeed!

Immediately they found themselves the centre of attraction, at least for the first couple of outings at their new base. However not everyone, they soon discovered, shared in their welcoming. There was a hierarchy to navigate, and it soon occurred that they had short-cutted this club tradition. Quickly, olive branches were offered, and a bit of grovelling got them further accepted into the mass.

'Clubs,' Jonny remarked to his skipper, after he had encountered the wrath of one of the club officials, 'scratch the surface and they are all a bit similar: golf, tennis, tiddly-winks - all the blomin same. Just as well we're out here on the water, well away from the pickiness, eh?' Richard nodded and he smiled in agreement, but for this trek, he hadn't gone looking to make early friends. His agenda was clear. In fact, other than Alan Burton, who had seconded their application, Paddy Duffy and a couple of other sailors they had made few, if any other acquaintances, never mind pals. But as Jonny reminded his skipper, having come to terms with his encounters: they'd only been members for five minutes.

'Right Jonny boy, as usual you're dead right. So, anyway; what's today's session all about?' The talking had stopped.

Thereafter they submerged themselves in the new facility; long hours of practice, often in solitary sail-abouts. They never missed an opportunity to get afloat or to compete, and it was paying off. Their new club's results board clearly evidenced (if evidence were needed) their steady progress up the rankings. They had earned themselves a place at the table, and as an aside their popularity within the membership was spreading too.

Other that a minority of 'jobs worth' type members their new base was providing them with not only excellent competition, but a beautiful back-drop. Although somewhat barren, the scenery was nevertheless dramatic. The reservoir seemed to sit on top of the world, a slow sweeping landscape of brown and green contrasted with acres of purple heather spreading away towards the horizons on all sides. In the summer when the water level sunk, their sailing area would be framed with a sandy border. Regardless of whenever the boys chose to sail there, there always seemed to be activity, whether it was other sailors, or fishing, or just sheep grassing down to the banks, they never felt alone.

An outright victory at the Welsh early season championship was snatched from club mates Alan Burton & Patrick Duffy at a windy Llandudno. This launched them into the top echelon of the fleet. Dave & Michael where undoubtedly tops overall and this guy John Simms still continued to rank at number two. Having actually beaten both Dave and Mr. Simms, what did that make them, they asked themselves? Too bloody big for our sailing boots, they quickly agreed.

Chapter Eleven

Finance!

The nationals, a solid week of racing, loomed ever nearer. It was no longer just a line drawn across their nautical year planner. Richard and Jonny inspected their echoing piggy banks yet again. Finally, they agreed that somehow they needed to raise extra finance. Entry fees, 'on the road' travelling expenses, entertainment costs (drink!) general maintenance and the constant replacement of gear had seriously eaten into their boat account. Their equipment had taken a battering. Being leading lights in the nautical sports world comes, they soon realised, with a price tag.

Top of the list – a complete suite of replacement sails: mainsail, two jibs and a spinnaker. It had been a predominately windy autumn and spring and their 'good' sails were, well, exhausted. If possible, and among a growing wish-list they were also keen to replace the existing spars. The good ship *Satisfaction* was generally looking a bit war-weary, not unlike their revenue pot.

'Look, Jonny,' said Richard, stating the obvious. 'With a mid-season mend-and-make-do refit we can make this boat sound and seaworthy. But without new sails we will be doing nothing more than pissing into the wind at Torquay. What's the point of even thinking we could take that title?' He was in the doldrums and on this occasion Jonny had no therapy to offer. Their evening at the local hostelry was a glum affair; even the beer tasted flat. They re-examined their options yet again.

It had been a long time since Richard and Jonny had a real boys' get-together. It seemed even longer since their last bender. They talked boats, relationships, families and friends, interspersed with music, cars, a little sport. But predictably every topic sooner or later returned them to their current predicament: finance, or the lack of it! The irony was that they knew exactly what to purchase, but an empty wallet held little clout. Nevertheless, they planned, dreamed...

The relatively new Southern Sail Making (SSM) loft, based in Kent near Whitstable harbour, had been the company consistently producing race-winning products of late. No wonder, as the boys had discovered. They were headed up by a partnership of three multi-championship-winning sailors. So all things being equal, this was the new logo on which their 1975 challenge would rest. But tough as it might be, they also agreed that without the investment it would be back to the day jobs. Being half-hearted and underpowered – agreeing, indeed, to be second best – was never an option. It remained an all-or-nothing strategy for this duo!

Acknowledging that their parents' generosity had allowed their adventure to be born, it was now down to them to keep it energised. The walk home from The Cellars that evening was long and sober, even though much beer and Bacardi had been sampled. Jonny stayed at Ashley Road that night...they talked into the early hours. There remained a determination not to be beaten, or least not to be beaten in public.

Richard's wage had certainly improved since joining the buying team. He was now taking home some £22.50 in a good week. But of course he had outgoings that left perhaps only half of this to play with. His impresario side-line, in the intensity of their sailing programme, had all but dried up. Because Jonny's studies were impacting heavily on his part-time bar work, his available contribution was now minimal. All in all a bit of an issue – a real ball-breaker if they were totally honest. Were they at a championship impasse? Becalmed and not even at the starting line?

During another after-work Cellars session with colleagues, Richard had laid bared their dilemma. He presented their credentials and opened his heart in a rousing and passionate address. Undeniably, he got his message across. They were right behind him!

No longer was sailing a girlie sport; in fact, a couple of the engineers had actually taken it up. There had been talk in the canteen of starting a sea society, although nothing came out of it.

It all seemed to come together in an instant. The bare bones of a Saturday night function, complete with raffle, was arranged in their honour. The venue, of course, would be The Cellars. Their recent successes appeared to have unlocked an unlikely local enthusiasm. If Richard had pitched this one correctly, the function might manifest itself in financial rescue, reinvigorating a wounded campaign. Of course for all of them, not least Richard and Jonny, it would also register an excuse for a long-overdue party.

Spontaneity requiring much organisation, there was much work to be done.

On the night it was shoulder-to-shoulder, and the girls were out in force too. Yes, it was a successful outing – financially as well! The Cellars was flooded with revellers. The pub consisted of a small L-shaped front room with a traditional bar running its length. But it was a bit of a Tardis. A second area lay five steps down. It was to the rear of the premises and was connected by a serving counter. Both levels were full to capacity. At the end of a wide corridor, which also led to a fairly new (and much-needed) toilet suite, the main function hall was reached.

The hall measured some100ft x 55ft, maybe more. It featured a sprung maple dance floor that had been reclaimed from an old school gymnasium. This was overlooked by a fully equipped stage hovering some three feet above the dance floor. At the opposite end of the hall a series of folding doors opened out onto a fashionable beer garden. The hall itself, which the Hepworth's acquired some years before as a disused warehouse, had brick walls to the eaves. It was capped with an insulated corrugated asbestos roof. For a time the 'shed' was used as a general store, a dumping area if the owners were honest, for their building business. In the late sixties, as the rock and pop boom seemed to just roll on and on, the structure came to represent a commercial opportunity.

After many months of toil, it emerged refurbished inside and out. Hardly betraying its previous existence, it now sat in sympathy with its surroundings. It was configured internally very much in harmony with The Cellars building itself, and quickly became established as a social hub of the town. Regular dances, concerts and black-tie events were proving to be a highly popular addition to the pub's portfolio.

The decor was clever and attractive. Roof, rafters and service units were all painted black, and from the darkness were suspended a series of magnificent 8' x 4' back-lit playing cards. They hovered over the dance floor, floating under a contrived night sky.

Rather than cladding the walls of bare cold brick with the usual panels of wood-effect beauty-board, the Hepworth's cleverly minimised the bleakness with a series of heavy dark drapes from eaves to floor, between which were hung large vertical abstracts depicting bar scenes and poker games. Down each side of the dance floor ran raised seating areas featuring candlelit tables. A clear view over the revellers added to the overall atmosphere. It was reminiscent of a western saloon and casino. The hall which acquired the nick-named of 'The Ranch' had also acquired a reputation for acoustics, a reputation which had spread out beyond the county. Performers, it seemed, queued up nightly, to experience the sounds and the ambience of the once, grotty old pub.

For the evening's entertainment Richard had called in a few favours. A couple of the bands he had previously managed answered his call. One of them, the Caroline Big Band, had hit the big time in the interim. His second choice, The Method, who would open the evening, were just getting noticed. Both bands, after submitting to their ex-manager's entreaties, agreed to play at cost to help stretch the sail fund a little further.

Playing his part on the night, Jonny stepped forward to act as master of ceremonies. Between the change-over of the bands he ran a short, sharp and financially rewarding auction and raffle. The money, it seemed, was rolling in.

Richard, however, his business brain characteristically engaged, was somewhat reticent. He was all too aware of the function's mounting tally of outgoings. Even at cost, he knew, top class entertainment doesn't come cheap: the musicians, door men, various other staff – all had to be paid. Altogether, there was a myriad of incidentals to cover. But he revelled in his management roll. He ensured that his team of helpers where operating efficiently around the venue – like a well-oiled machine. He also found time to enjoy the music and muse at his own talent-spotting ability, and not only the music...

Penny, in her role as Jonny's assistant, turned out to be the weak link in the chain. Although Jonny shielded her, his buddy could see that she was somewhat swamped. Life outside college, it seemed, ran at a quicker pace. But as Richard said, nobody died... Not only was the target raised but the piggy bank left unopened. The shackles, suddenly, had fallen away, allowing their dream to be reborn. Completed with a new urgency, their purchase-orders and deposits for the essential equipment got despatched the following week.

A week or so later Richard took a telephone call at his desk in the open-plan buyer's office. The receptionist, much to his annoyance, had once again patched the caller through to his extension without an introduction. Believing it to be either a supplier or a cold caller, he nevertheless answered.

'Good morning, Richard D'Arcy speaking. Can I help?'

Some confusion followed, before the penny dropped. He had been caught unawares and asked the caller bluntly, 'How did you get this number?' He was more flustered than annoyed. It turned out that his mother, taking a call at Ashley Road, had decided it was important enough to give out her son's works number. Company policy discouraged private calls. Believing he was under the gaze of the entire office he quickly balanced the pros and cons. He, too, privately deemed the call important enough to proceed. After all, he thought, this could be life-changing – it's not every day that your sail maker calls...

The caller had already re-introduced herself as Tracey from Southern and was in the midst of her spiel, congratulating him on his recent form, when Richard interrupted, asking her to hold. He explained that he was going to transfer the call. 'It'll only take a moment,' he said. 'Please bear with me.' Tracey agreed. The call was transferred to his supervisor's office – Jim Jones was on a day's leave. The closed door would offer the privacy this conversation would require. I don't need, he thought, to share my life with the world at large. Lifting the phone he signalled to Lucy at the next-door desk to replace the receiver. She did so, and he closed Jim's door.

'Hello, hello Tracey. Can you hear me?'

He sat on the edge of Jim's desk, and pushed a pile of invoices away to make space for his A4 notepad.

'Yes Mr. D'Arcy, I can hear you fine.' She continued in well-practiced and rather posh southern tones before transferring Richard to the technical director of Southern Sail Making. There followed a question and answer session. The SSM man wanted to confirm final measurements and other details before they commenced 'the build' of *Satisfaction's* new sail wardrobe. The call took some fifteen minutes, but Richard wasn't counting. Afterwards he stood up, gazed down on Jim's unkempt desk and proclaimed aloud:

'Jeez: A personalised service or what? Jonny was right, we have made the news, and down south too!'

Before returning to his desk he rang Jonny. As he relayed the conversation he confided that some of the questions the guy asked – he couldn't remember his name – were somewhat over his head. Jonny put it a little more pointedly.

'You hadn't a notion what he was talking about, had you mate?'

There was a pause, but no response. Richard just smiled to himself. Jonny, remembering Samantha's comments when they had met at the hospital, broke the silence.

'He probably assumed that you were an expert.' Richard didn't rise to that bait either but changed the subject to Aston Villa's current form... before returning to his work, smiling.

Thirty-one days before the nationals the SSM delivery arrived. They had already picked up their replacement spars some weeks previously from the same chandlery where the infamous paint debate took place.

Suddenly their campaign had been elevated from a shadow chasing adventure. The D'Arcy-Dubois Sailboat Team realised, probably for the first time, that they had 'the ammunition' at their disposal. For a moment Richard and Jonny got really quite serious and nervous; even Richard had realised and with some embarrassment, became a little emotional. Reality, like a runaway bus, had hit them both. A high five the spontaneous acceptance.

'You know Richard,' Jonny announced 'It's not just you me and the folks anymore, no.' He paused. 'Now that we've gone public, all those people who contributed to the fund-raiser will be watching us, and expecting a result too!' Richard gritted his teeth, summarised the state of the finances, and grunted that other people's expectations were the last thing he needed reminded of.

'What is it with you anyway?' he said. 'Don't you think we have enough to worry about?' Then he immediately apologised. 'Sorry mate, think it's all got to me.' Jonny smiled. With their event entry form and entrance fee (kindly donated by the Hepworth's) in the post, their campaign was now official. The countdown had commenced. There was no going back.

Chapter Twelve

A Campaigning Strategy

Other than distilling data on how to maximise their new purchases, three key areas focused their attention: the journey to Devon, accommodation and catering, and the racing and race area itself.

Torbay was a new venue for the fleet. Advice on even the best route was in short supply. Information on the likely conditions they would face down there was non-existent. Only two other teams from their club had elected to enter for this year's championship. Although disappointing, it was understandable; there remained a general nervousness: industrial unrest, the bad taste of three-day-week, fuel and other shortages, and of course, Northern Ireland. It was a dire time. Although elevated somewhat from the realities, the boys found it hard at times to reconcile their sporting quest with the everyday hardships being faced by their neighbours, and indeed many of their friends. Also victim of the times, their new club was not to be represented down south in quantity this time around, but nevertheless it would be draped, three ways, in quality.

Paul Owen, a 35-year-old physical education teacher his crew, 20-year-old Laura Graham, a secretary, were the current Midlands champions. Unsurprisingly, they had entered. So too had 19-year-old Alan Burton. He was a student of fine art. His crew for the week was Patrick Duffy, the local plumber. They were not a regular pairing but young Al was fast becoming a bit of a lad to watch. Some reckoned he could be the new champion. Given the right conditions, in fact, both of these teams were very capable of winning. There was an air of confidence and expectation in their new home camp. D'Arcy & Dubois were in good company.

The journey seemed simple enough at first glance. But a deeper study of the BP map of the day revealed it as something of an expedition – the championship was some 280 miles away, one way: Torbay may have been the English Rivera, but it wasn't the easiest of venues to get to from 'up north', especially in August.

Fuel consumption was a critical issue. Just how many extra gallons would towing the boat consume, both ways? Then there was the weight of all the gear and its effect on miles per gallon: spares, the week's living supplies, not forgetting their wardrobe, afloat and shore-side. The budget was revisited yet again. It was not, they agreed, a crisis.

Richard and Jonny were immediately minded of one of their previous season's outings. More a calamity than an outing. They lost the offside wheel from the trailer; actually, and to their horror, it overtook them as they braked for a bend in the road. With a degree of mechanical ingenuity they just about retrieved the situation but missed out on a full day's racing. A more painful experience followed; the time they failed to make it home on a Sunday evening. They didn't queue early enough for petrol and paid the price. The sleepover on a isolated garage forecourt, awaiting a tanker delivery, was not pleasant. Neither was the goading Richard had to endure from his workmates.

This was to be their longest and undoubtedly most prestigious trek yet. They needed to be organised. Their rig – towing vehicle, trailer and other associated equipment – needed to be mechanically sound. The journey had become as much of a challenge as the championship itself. Those early seventies had been difficult for eventing. Turnouts at the key events seemed to reflect the pervading atmosphere of social unrest and low national morale. But this scenario had converted into a positive for D'Arcy & Dubois. Facing the cream of the fleet at regatta after regatta had provided them with an opportunity to fast-track up the rankings.

Richard's dad was a dab hand at DIY and the gardening stuff, but when it came to things mechanical he, like his son, was mystified. Hearing of their dilemma, Arthur's brother Jim, a car mechanic, came to the rescue. His offer of engineering expertise plus the loan of his pristine and beloved VW campervan were accepted without hesitation. No thought of the financial implications was entertained at the time, but later a dithering Richard asked of Jonny:

'Is this a luxury? Can we afford it?'

Another visit to the budget confirmed they could, just. No longer a luxury item, the campervan was considered vital equipment. Uncle Jim, like his nephew, was a motoring enthusiast. The only difference was that he actually knew about the things that mattered: route planning, servicing, mechanics...

It had just gone 8:30 on a Saturday morning. The VW stood proudly in Ashley Road. By lunchtime their boat trailer was inspected and passed as roadworthy. In the process Jim had discovered that the entire suspension was, as he put it, 'living on a wing and a prayer!'

His visit coincided with the arrival of Jonny in his dad's new(ish) Volvo Estate. Uncle Jim, very much in his element, was taking no chances. Although its dark blue livery looked classic, it moved him not at all. He had the bonnet up quicker, in his own words, that a gust under Marilyn's skirt. His eyes darted with curiosity. He proceeded to spread his magic mechanical dust over its engine compartment, soon declaring it, too, fit for purpose.

It was a wonderful weekend all round. The brothers – Arthur and Jim – had not spent real time together for years. Richard drove his uncle back home to Derby on the Sunday evening. Uncle Jim's instructions on extracting top performance from the VW may have laboured somewhat, but Richard didn't complain – how could he?

With the route established and the equipment roadworthy, the next task concerned the healthy living strategy. Previously at regattas they had pitched a couple of tents. They would snack: pie and chip takeaways, chocolate and, of course, beer. That was the norm. Sometimes when the weather was seriously inclement (or they had, as Jonny always said, 'drink taken') they even camped out on a club house floor. This time, however, it had to be different.

With king-sized portions of maturity, Richard and Jonny knew that to be in the running for the title they must maintain a consistent level, not just of fitness, but of mental alertness too. Going afloat with a hangover or a dodgy stomach would not win a race series. To this end, Richard had taken to training with the factory's rugby league team. He also was eating salad – with his chips. The results were noticeable. Jonny, for his part, continued to encourage his skipper…

Of course the state that reigning champion Dave Gilmour, with increasing frequency, could get into before a race could easily chase away Richard's new thinking. Dave's drinking had become more pronounced this season. Other sailors had noticed it too; a bit of a worry, they all agreed, for such a likeable bloke.

Their revised plan involved using the VW as the main sleeping accommodation. Richard's sister's large continental tent would act as a larder, cooking room, workshop and drying area. Jonny's small tent could be used as back-up. Penny had already signalled that she was unlikely to travel down to Devon. Richard couldn't resist a quick goad.

'You're free man for a week then, Jonny boy.' He just got one of his stares back.

To avoid the risk of damaging *Satisfaction* en route, it was agreed that the VW and the Volvo should take the strain. Penny's healthy food menu amounted to a catering regime – for a family of ten. As a luck penny, the local grocer even gave some discount.

The final task, and for the boys the most important, was to understand the vagaries of the likely race venue. Jonny took the lead on this. He had amassed a plethora of contacts. This included David Robinson, whose business card he had reserved for just such an occasion. The ensuing discussion provided him with a checklist of absolutes: a chart of the bay, tide tables, and contact details for any sailors (Penny's old skipper, for example) who had previous experience of the venue.

Finally – ideally – he needed to source a knowledgeable local. Jonny soon had it all sorted, with the exception of that 'wise old local'. A week to go and they were actually organised. They had even met up with Andy Thompson, Penny's skipper – he was in fact very helpful. He had competed there in '71 finished in the top ten, albeit without Penny. They didn't dare remind her of this, but they agreed to file it for further use...

Chapter Thirteen

The Expedition...

The Big Boss had summoned Richard on the Friday morning. His secretary, Mrs Greenwood, was not famed for her sense of humour.

'Mr D'Arcy please come to…'

Apprehensive, Richard tentatively measured every step along a dull corridor; he was preparing his excuses. He was expecting a rollicking, but a timid knock on Joe Martin's open door was answered with a cheery, 'Good mornin' young fella! S'pose you're wondering why I called you up here at such an unearthly hour?'

Before Richard had time to muster a mature reply, Joe Martin had his hand outstretched. With an air of enthusiasm he confirmed that the long-awaited promotion had come through. This was a relief more than a surprise. Richard was very conscious of the fact that he had been spending more company time on the expedition than on the business that paid his (albeit lowly) wages...

Joe Martin was the senior purchasing manager. He was a no-nonsense type of leader, tending to remain somewhat distant, though never aloof. He quietly kept a finger on the office pulse. Although his office looked out onto the business floor he would seldom be seen watching his team through the windowed wall. Instead of presenting Richard with a disciplinary note he followed the formals by wishing them every success for the week ahead. He had caught Richard off-guard; he had never considered for a moment that his post-work exploits would be of any interest to management, especially to someone at Mr Joe Martin's level in the hierarchy.

Joe went on to intimate that with the bad old days of the three-day-week behind them, company growth plans would soon be revealed. Richard listened. He listened as intently as the distraction of the journey ahead would allow. Joe carried on between sips of coffee from a stained Newcastle United mug. He intimated that the competitiveness and obvious organisational talent his young buyer had demonstrated were just the personal traits that any company would be looking for in career-minded staff.

Richard's attention was re-ignited. Repositioned on the edge of his chair, he clasped his hands between his knees, in anticipation, his mind racing.

Flippin 'eck. Am I being singled out as management material?

Unaccountably, he stood up. Suddenly he felt alone and vulnerable. Turning to his left, across the circular conference table, he focused his attention on his colleagues through the blinds on the windowed wall. Heads were either down shifting paper or phones were trapped between shoulders and ears. The day's business had clicked into gear. He suddenly yearned to be a part of it. Trying to select a meaningful way to thank his leader for his kind words, he just stood there. He felt unable to express his gratitude. Curiously, in that moment of hesitation – it seemed like an eternity – he couldn't help noticing how pristine and orderly this office was kept. It was the opposite of the annex in which his direct supervisor, Jim Jones, squatted.

This is how my office would look, he dreamed...

'Oh, and by the way.' Joe smiled broadly at Richard, who was already edging towards the door. 'You can get away at noon today. It'll help you miss some of that damned holiday traffic – good luck and bring back some silverware.'

Flippin 'eck, he thought again, closing Joe's door. Nothing like putting pressure on a chap. The corridor somehow seemed lighter and shorter now. He couldn't contain his delight. The grin was his give-away; A 'good morning' and a topical comment even brought a hint of a smile to Mrs Greenwoods normally sour face! In those passing minutes he yearned for someone to ask why he had been called up into the big office...

To say that Richard was ecstatic would be an understatement. He was to discover later that the managing director, Charles Whitworth, and a couple of the southern-based board members were also keen sailors, and he wondered if news of his endeavours would filter up to their Bristol headquarters. Perhaps he *was* being watched after all. He was ahead of himself again, but he didn't care – he had only one thing on his mind.

Richard telephoned Jonny from a desk that was being hastily tidied to advise him of the revised timetable. Jonny, however, was already on the starting blocks; had been since breakfast. The Volvo was fully fuelled, the boat was securely hitched and the rig sat poised and prominent on his Stafford driveway awaiting the off

The clock was ticking, and at exactly 11:50 a.m. the office went silent. Jim, Richard's supervisor, emerged from his 'cave' to summon the twelve-strong buying team. After a few kind words of encouragement – he may have been a supportive supervisor and a clever buyer but he, like Richard, was no speechmaker – he handed over a signed Good Luck card plus a cash donation.

Richard, in reply, and with a quivering bottom lip, thanked the little gathering for their kindness. He told them sincerely that they – he and Jonny – would do their best. He noticed Sarah peeping through the glazed door panel. He nodded; she smiled and mouthed 'good luck'.

It was now just after five to. Jim told him to be off. Sarah was off too. Two steps at a time and he was on the ground floor. Richard D'Arcy had exited the building. He was indeed into the Sprite and off – or would have been. His acceleration was a bit premature. Too much choke. The engine flooded.

'Damn, damn! Right Richard, calm yourself, let's think this through,' he said, between gritted teeth. He knew full well that he had an audience at the first floor window. Using less choke and a little more delicate accelerator pedal work the Sprite fired back into life amid a cloud of blue exhaust fumes. There was an overpowering smell of petrol. He did, however, manage to burn some rubber as he exited the factory gate.

And so the expedition had begun. First the homeward jaunt to exchange his soft-top for the VW camper – then the adventure would commence for real!

Transfer complete and after the obligatory hugs, kisses and well-wishes from his folks, siblings, nieces and nephews, Richard and pre-loaded campervan were finally away.

The drive to Jonny's house, a rather splendid detached red brick dwelling set in a quarter acre of leafy grounds on the boundary of Stafford, allowed him time to gather his thoughts. It was a much-needed quiet moment after the mayhem at Ashley Road and the office.

Having reversed down into the driveway and up to the Volvo's front bumper, Richard joined Jonny and they went over the final checklist together. They ensured that nothing was forgotten or left behind.

They were done and itching to get away... when Jonny's mother Lillian and his Nan Nancy introduced an entirely new agenda. They absolutely insisted the pair eat a proper lunch before departure.

At 14:00 hours exactly, the *Satisfaction* convoy finally rolled out of town; destination Torbay the English resort of Devon and the 1975 National Sailing Championship.

Two-and-three-quarter hours driving later, the Volvo, which now led the convoy, indicated left and rolled into a filling station and adjoining cafe. After refuelling both vehicles, they rechecked that their mistress had remained securely seated on her trailer. Then they treated themselves to a much-anticipated pee and retired to the cafe for refreshments and a stretch.

The going, although a bit slow, had been steady. They were more or less on schedule and more especially, revived. His uncle's route notes were proving exemplary.

'Mate, remember I said that I'd keep an eye out for the mysterious Samantha?' announced Jonny without warning. Adopting an instant meerkat stance, Richard was immediately engaged.

'Well,' he continued in his annoying drawl, 'it turns out that she lives in the Torquay area and works in the local hospital down there. I was talking to...'

'Never mind who you were talking to,' Richard interrupted. 'Will she be around during this event?' Jonny quickened his delivery.

'Look skipper, all I know is that her mother died last year after a long illness, and that's the reason she hasn't been seen around the circuit – that really is all I know, mate.'

'Well now Jonny boy.' Richard, looking heavenwards, was grinning like the proverbial Cheshire. 'That'll occupy my thoughts for next spell of driving the van – have you ever driven one of those bloody things?'

'Just you keep your eyes on the tarmac and focus on that boat ahead of you, you little love-struck dickhead,' said Jonny.

'And there was me thinking you were still pining after Sarah, the super-babe.'

'I saw her today. She waved, smiled. Wished me luck.'

'You're something else mate; you're a dreamer. She blew *you* out, remember?' Richard paused, looked at him and smiled, thinking: never say never…

'Oh, and yes,' – Jonny took up the story again – 'Samantha said she *will* meet us there, so focus R-i-c-k-y...'

'Oh Jonny, you can be so masterful at times.' Richard punched Jonny's shoulder, sniggering, but Jonny retaliated with a slap on the back which damned near put him into the VW's driver's seat, without opening the door!

'Jeez, I hope you've enough of that aggression to last for the whole week; you're an animal.'

'I haven't even started yet, mate.'

'Hey, and you a single man again too...' This produced a Jonny stare.

After navigating Bristol and the horrors of the obligatory holiday traffic, they had Exeter in their sights. Then there it was; the first sign for Torquay. In the rapidly descending dusk the outline of Torbay was next. Perhaps the most welcoming of all vistas, it provided both of them with an injection of adrenalin. It was not only uplifting but it rebuilt the level of expectation and excitement. After hundreds of miles and hours of watching black tarmac curving left and right, Richard's eyes were hollowed and red-rimmed, while Jonny had taken to continuous yawning. Both drivers had reached the end of their endurance cycle. Following Uncle Jims final note they pulled over at a strategically placed roadside watering hole. They needed to establish and indeed agree on how the hell they were going to find the designated championship camp site. It was located somewhere out on the other side of Torquay. That stop also provided a necessary rest. If nothing else it allowed some life to be injected into numb bums and seized limbs. This really had been a ball-breaking, nay, ball-squashing expedition; over six bloody hours, and they were still not there.

'Thank goodness for the Uncle Jims of this world,' said Richard. 'No dodgy trailers or spluttering engines this time, eh Jonny boy?'

He promised himself he would telephone his uncle as soon as they were settled – well, after apprising the folks of their safe arrival in Devon.

They needn't have worried about directions. It was clearly signposted and besides, there seemed to be hoards of other boats on trailers heading their way. Having located the championship venue the duo – now feeling a bit cocky –easily found the nearby campsite. The hat trick was claiming their designated parking spot, first time.

It was now dark. They were dog-tired. They unhitched the 'mistress', parked up and levelled the VW as best they could. Jonny popped up the roof, pulled out the double bunk, and then drove them down to the host club.

They registered. They phoned the folks. Hellos were uttered to various people – a combination of club volunteers and fellow competitors. They downed a pint of Witney's Red Barrel each and retreated back to the site, turning in, knackered.

Chapter Fourteen

A Time for Reflection?

It was no longer a dream. They had actually arrived in Devon. Torbay had yet to fully reveal itself. It was a somewhat over-excited Richard who laid his head that night. He had been hyper, his head buzzing with excitement and expectation. It had been building all day, and sleep was to be short-lived.

Like a spring, he found himself bolt upright in the darkness of his bunk. He was awash with sweat, breathing heavily. Confused, he found himself in a mild panic. He tried to get his bearings.

His dream – nightmare – had reared up luminous from the serenity of his slumber. This was not an unusual occurrence. But it had been a long time since he had suffered a similar attack. Sudden awakenings – leftover reactions from a troubled youth, underpinned by self-consciousness – were something from which Richard thought he had escaped. Now, they threatened the positives of recent days.

This was a bad one. It was as if he had been catapulted back to childhood. Suddenly, he was reliving those early days. The taunts and the trials. School was a period that Richard had blocked from his psyche. But occasionally, usually in times of high stress, it had a tendency to surface without warning. For this occasion, it presented itself in spectacular fashion. This was indeed a bad one.

Upright and rigid in the pre-dawn, he saw that it was just gone three: only the luminous hands of his wristwatch provided any indication of time or place. He was wide-awake now. Eyes selective, adjusting. The buzzing in his head, and the visions, wouldn't go away. He sat there for what seemed like an eternity. He was alone; he was boy.

Mindful not to disturb Jonny, peacefully unconscious beside him, he carefully removed himself from the sleeping bag. With ankles hooked over the bunk end he pulled himself carefully and in silence he dropped onto his knees. Fumbling around the floor he slipped on his jeans and a t-shirt.

Silently he opened the van door but clipped his little toe on a corner – couldn't utter a sound. The pain! Stepping down into the stillness of the night, the cool and dampness of the grass seemed to absorb the throbbing, and gradually his eyes began to function. Only the sodium glare of a distant lamp light broke up the black ceiling.

No moon, no stars. No sound – well, other than romantic athletics emanating from a nearby tent. Richard smiled. He knew exactly who she was.

As he sat there on an upturned bucket it seemed that nothing could distract from his memory recoil. The images persisted, commanding him to submit, no matter how much his heart objected.

His primary years, he supposed, were OK. Mostly fun and mischievous, albeit tempered by one particularly nasty teacher. He had come to believe that she 'got off' on applying the cane. In times of stress Miss Savage – whose moral compass, he often thought, had somehow been calibrated according to the accident of her name – would frequently appear in his nightmare. But he became able for her. He developed the habit of mentally re-dressing her, ogre-style. He ventured a thin smile.

What the young Richard lacked in brain power he made up for in playground credibility. He was by no means a bully, but in mixing with what would later become 'the wrong crowd' he learnt how to defend himself. He was one of the smaller boys. Nevertheless, he soon earned the badge of respect; he was not a boy to be picked on. Maybe he was just lazy. Maybe more misguided than mum and dad D'Arcy had realised. Perhaps it was the dyslexia that was diagnosed many years later. But the climax of his primary school years was the dramatic failure of the 11-Plus exam.

So instead of routing via grammar school towards academia, as had been the family tradition, it was off to the local secondary modern for young Richard. There followed a parental culture shift. To their great disappointment a similar educational pattern followed: poor school work and a drop-off in general interest levels. Home reports revealed a troubling taste for truancy.

As if things were not bad enough for his exasperated parents, to their utter disgust worse was to follow. Richard's mother Molly innocently answered the kitchen telephone on a pleasant summer's afternoon.

'Sergeant Lynch here....'

Molly was grateful for the stool positioned alongside the breakfast bar. The call revealed that a cocky young D'Arcy, who by then had become a fully paid-up member of the same 'bad company', had now discovered the wrath of the law! Only on the interjection of his father, a partner in a local firm of accountants, did he avoid proceedings; how this came to be was never spoken of, then or since.

Frog-marched out of the local police station by his father, he neither spoke nor was spoken to on the short drive home. However, as the stained glass front door closed, the temperature rose as the atmosphere cooled.

Richard found himself being propelled on his backside up the hallway sliding over the faux wood linoleum. He ended up crumpled against the downstairs toilet door. His father, in pursuit, was removing his belt... Till the day he died, he thought, he would never forget those burning eyes of anger.

Hurt and exasperated, the normally placid Arthur D'Arcy was not a violent man – the opposite in fact. Often it was Molly who dished out the chastising. This time, however, Richard had stepped across the line. All the values his parents preached had, it seemed, been very publicly flushed away that afternoon. At the end of his tether, father D'Arcy grabbed his son by his collar. With a fist of cloth he was lifted, toes paddling for grip. A loud slap resonated down the hall, followed by another. Arthur shouted:

'WHY?'

Molly, in shock, had never seen her husband so angry. She was now screaming at Arthur to stop. She tried to get between them.

As Richard attempted to escape to his room, a polished brown brogue connected squarely with his rear-end. It lifted him two clear steps up the carpeted stairway and came with a verbal accompaniment.

'Yes, get you up to your room... and stay there!' Arthur, himself now crying, issued his final condemnation.

'You're a disgrace. How could you, how could you be so stupid. How could you dishonour your family – this is not finished, not by a long way.'

Molly was still shouting at her husband; he couldn't hear her. With bowed head shielding reddened eyes, he grabbed a jacket. He slammed the front door, stormed down the paved garden path, kicked the wrought iron gate open and was gone. He didn't return for three hours.

Shaking uncontrollably in the night air, Richard remembered vividly how the pain had shot up his 'tail'. He recalled being crouched on the floor with his knees bent up tightly into his chest. He had jammed himself securely between the edge of his bed and the wall, and he sobbed relentlessly. He reverted to a more comfortable, foetal position. He hid under the flower patterned blue sheets. Mother was sent away a number of times with a tearful 'NO.'

The D'Arcy household, as he remembered, remained a very tense and quiet residence for what seemed an eternity. Yes, there had been uproars concerning his older siblings before, but this was different. This was really scary. Richard had never witnessed such anger at home. He had never seen his parents so outraged, and at each other. He remained confined to his room for more than a week, even allowing his 'release' day to pass. His time, he remembered, was spent strumming the guitar, drawing and playing mostly singles on a black and grey Dansette record player. He had finally come to understand the enormity of his crime. OK, the shoplifting was bad. But it was worse because he got caught. Nothing could have prepared him for the effect it had on the family unit.

Cast aside and alone, he remembered vividly the hopelessness of his situation. He didn't know what to do or which way to turn. He remained a lost soul. During his incarceration he neither washed nor fully dressed. Many of his meals were returned untouched. He felt unloved, unwanted and all but abandoned by the family.

In the cool and quiet of that Devon night, Richard recalled as if it were yesterday his final proclamation, having convinced himself that there was no way out for him.

'I've really pushed it too far, so best if I just disappear, run off. Perhaps I should even rejoin the gang – at least they respect me. As for school, who's going to miss me?'

Arthur, too, was suffering mentally. The 'quiet treatment' being administered by Molly served only to deepen the pain, and continued to erode his self-esteem. Finally, some days later it all came to ahead. He rose sharply from the isolation of another silent dinner, pushed his picked-over meal away across a gingham patterned table cloth and declared:

'ENOUGH, this has to end!' He climbed the stairs purposefully, leaving Molly at the first step, looking up.

'You lay another finger...'

He cut her off. 'That's enough. I said, that's enough!'

Richard remembered well the footsteps on the landing, the quiet knock on his door. It was opened tentatively to reveal the framed silhouette of his father. He remembered dropping his packed duffle bag over the edge of his single bed; reverting to the knees-into-chest defence posture; backing rapidly into the headboard.

He couldn't remember every detail of the ensuing conversation. But he could see his dad sitting down beside him, quietly explaining, and apologising for *his* actions on that dark day. He could still feel his dad embracing him, comforting him. He remembered promising never to be 'bad' again. He heard himself sobbing.

'Dad I'm really sorry. I'll make it up to everyone, I will.'

He barely heard his father's soft reply.

'I know, I know, let's just leave it all in the past son, we'll do this together.'

Richard had never forgotten those words, nor the kiss on his forehead, the welling up in his dad's eyes.

Whether it was the shock of being awakened to the realities of life, or the bodily aches, Richard had turned a corner. He was entering his fourth term and his education record, for all the wrong reasons, remained a highlight of his school years. But, with a significant degree of one-to-one tutoring, the dying embers of academic endeavour were somehow re-ignited. The glow unearthed a dormant talent for mathematics. In English, however, he never made the grade. In the end he left school at sixteen with a reasonable portfolio of vocational certificates – enough to allow the next career step to be planned.

With some covert assistance the young D'Arcy was to become an office junior at a nearby manufacturing concern. Soon, he demonstrated a new energy. In his second year he was drafted into the offices of procurement, and the rest, he realised, was history... Socially, too, his outlook changed. He and his father, now great friends cemented their involvement at the nearby sailing and fishing club; Father purchased a second-hand dinghy.

Richard's sailing career begun. The fascination with boats and the sea, which had occupied his pre-teens, had re-emerged, and family holidays in Mumbles were a case in point. During their week he could frequently be found fixated by the sight of sailboats line abreast on the beach. In readiness for launching into the surf, their sails would be flapping and crackling. He was utterly absorbed. Equally, and within the sanctuary of his own company, he could be found glued to his dad's binoculars, hypnotised by armadas of bellowing spinnakers out in the bay.

The explosion of the sixties made its impact on the young Richard. Indeed, for a time it brought about a 180-degree turnaround, dampening his aquatic interests. Richard answered the call of another Great Adventure: music, fashion; and girls.

It was now approaching four in the morning, and greyness bordered the night sky. Richard suddenly realised that he was freezing; physically shaking. He quickly retreated to the warmth of the van and disappeared into his sleeping bag – didn't bother removing his clothes...

Chapter Fifteen

The Championship Begins

Saturday dawned bright and breezy; too breezy to contemplate a trial sail out in the bay. The day was therefore given over to various mundane tasks: unpacking, washing (the boat) rigging, tuning, as well as setting up home for the week; not to mention getting the lay of the land and catching up on sleep. This was interspersed with numerous conversations with co-competitors and the very welcoming folk from the club.

Their pitch had become the focal point for their club mates. Dave, Michael and Julian, who arrived around midday, joined the impromptu party. Apart from the swirling wind the day was warm, the company relaxed. Banter flowed and without warning it was mid-afternoon...

Jonny had a special surprise awaiting his skipper. As well as all his championship preparations he had also unearthed that 'wise old local'. It turned out that his tutor's brother was a leading light in the nearby Royal Devon Maritime Club's Dragon fleet of yachts.

As the others took their leave, the plump outline of their 'local' emerged from a beat-up and faded blue Land Rover and homed in on their stand, Richard turned to Jonny and commented:

'Bloody hell, you do move in elevated circles these days. Firm handshakes followed. The kettle was duly filled and replaced on the burner – they had transferred all the van's cooking facilities to the adjacent tent. All three now retired to the VW for a personalised briefing.

After qualifying, Archie MacArthur had moved down there some years ago. He had joined a dental practice in Torquay. During his university years he was heavily involved in the sport's 'team racing circuit' and competed regularly in its famous Wilson Trophy at West Kirby's Marine Lake near Liverpool. His recent sailing activity, for some number of years, had been in larger boats, most recently the afore named Dragon class of yacht.

Jonny understood that Archie was no slouch around the bay. He liked this little Scotsman, with his enormous ginger beard, balding head and his infectious enthusiasm. He meticulously worked the boys through every square inch of their Torbay chart. He regaled them with stories, and with tales of his yachting achievements – naturally, with epic victories from his university sailing days. Recently, it appeared, he had been victorious at the local Regatta Week.

The boys were suitably impressed. But were they wise to put so much trust in someone who in reality, albeit warm, welcoming and generous, was a total stranger? He was, after all, very much a self-appointed expert. After an hour or so, and several cuppas, Jonny called time on the session. It was an attempt to find some fresh air: Archie's pipe had created a leaden ceiling so thick that it had descended to eye level. Richard and Jonny had recently stopped smoking. They decided to finish the briefing in the large tent they had erected earlier alongside the VW. The session now at its hyperbolic climax, an animated summary was accompanied by a few wee drams that Archie had magically produced.

'Is that the time?' said Archie. 'I need to get back.'

He paused, turning to the boys.

'Maybe you'd like a wee sail this evening. Just to get you acquainted, you know, with the waters?'

'Seriously?' the boys said in unison.

'Ay-ee, no time like the present – come on laddies, grab a spray top and hop in.'

They jumped into the Land Rover and headed off round the bay to the Maritime Club.

How the other half live, Richard said to himself, then his mind drifted back to that posh training day... *You hypocrite*, he thought.

The aged and rattling Land Rover, encouraged by a somewhat gung-ho driving style, interrupted the easy flow of conversation as Archie wrestled it towards their destination. It wasn't that the vehicle had any serious turn of speed, it was that Archie seemed determined to maintain a constant speed regardless of the road shape or surface. Passengers, thought Richard, needed to be lashed down, and his thoughts inevitably drifted back to Penny's driving style...

With the wind abated, the sail in Archie's Dragon was both educational and effortless, unlike the drive they had just endured. The Dragon just seemed to glide through the seaway and over the waves left from the earlier gale.

The main purpose of the voyage was not, however, to cruise in the early evening Devon sun, pleasant as it was. No, the purpose was to translate Archie's briefing into tangible way-points and landmarks. From these, Richard and Jonny could identify any wind bends, wind changes, and tidal movements which might occur during the forthcoming series of championship races. Basically, Richard wanted himself and Jonny to become locals for the week ahead. They were absolutely overjoyed with Archie's support and told him so as they sailed homeward. The huge red spinnaker ballooned towards the harbour. They believed that he was appreciative too. All hoped that they had created a win/win scenario.

112

As time had drifted away, very much like the wind, they elected to head back to the championship village rather than retiring to the plush surroundings of the club lounge – not like them to turn down an invitation. Archie transferred his guests to the care of another club member who was heading for Dartmouth.

Cind's pristine red S-type Jaguar provided them with a luxurious return journey. She was the wife of the club's sailing captain and one of Archie's crew members. A lady both boys reckoned to be in her early forties, though her fresh tanned complexion might have suggested younger. Blond and tall, she was extremely attractive. Her tight white skirt and black top made no attempt to disguise a trim figure. Conversation flowed – sailing tittle-tattle mostly. In the passenger seat, Richard couldn't help making a quiet appraisal from behind his sunglasses. Jonny, being that bit taller, was able to survey her cleavage from the vantage point of the back seat. She, of course, was well aware of the situation, but she continued maturely to converse and to drive ... She could vouch, she said, for their mentor's credentials.

Their journey terminated all too soon. Chauffeur Cindy politely declined their offer of an evening cocktail. So for them a couple of relaxing pints loomed, and soon they felt at home in the club. It turned out to be a few pints plus.

The competitors' natural curiosity, together with the ambience of the venue, turned the evening into one big party night. It was a great start to a championship week, both boys agreed. At an opportune moment, however, they both quietly slipped away. They were determined to be good boys that week. And Richard's troubled sleep pattern had finally rendered him knackered.

Chapter Sixteen

Championship prologue...

While Jonny was happily snoring away, his decibel level vibrating the VW'S many attachments, the skipper's insomnia had returned. He relished his promotion; sailed the course in his mind's eye; relived the evening's entertainment. But mostly Richard wondered if the mysterious and much-missed Samantha would indeed make her promised appearance. He needed to sleep. It was a going to be big day tomorrow...

1: New Day Dawning

.... A shaft of brilliant Devon sunlight wrenched Richard from his dreams. Showtime was upon them! Actually it was breakfast time. Jonny arose bright and breezy, and was well organised in the catering department.

The host sailing club and venue for the championship was located more or less in the centre of the arc of the bay. The official notice board confirmed that eighty-three boats were entered for the championship. That converted to 166 competitors plus family, friends and supporters, together with the hoards of club volunteers: enough enthusiasts to make the event happen and run smoothly.

It was, thought Richard, a real championship village; not at all like anything from the last year. It was all that he had expected – or hoped for. It was as if he had been transported from the gloom and the grey of the north for a moment in the sun. His mind momentarily considered the debated divides between the north and the south. It all seemed so real in that moment... He breathed hard, turned and surveyed the surroundings.

Richard was a sucker for detail, and as he assessed the set-up his eyes danced around the site, alighting on the row of flagpoles: *flippin 'eck, it's dressed like a mini Olympics*! Following his private thought path, he could immediately see why the club's grounds had been transformed into a tented village. The clubhouse itself, although quite modern, was compact. A huge white central marquee had been erected on what must have been the car park. It now formed the hub of the event, overshadowing the clubhouse, a single-storey brick-built structure with a mono-pitched slate roof, Bangor Blues he surmised.

The prickly matter of changing and toilet requirements had, he noticed, been cleverly addressed with a portable suite of facilities. The male changing area was generously extended by abutting a small blue-and white-striped marquee to the clubhouse.

'You know something,' he said aloud, 'this is all very slick; these guys really know what they're doing'. Richard was no longer, he thought, a lad who could rough it with any degree of ease. He'd experienced too many events where the toilet facilities outshone the main event.

Suddenly he became aware that the competitors were being summoned to the official championship opening and briefing. The formal welcomes were followed by introductions to key personnel and sponsors. Then it was the handing over of pennants – club to class association, then class association to host club. It rolled on. The competitors were itching to get afloat. After a series of drawn-out and dreary speeches, the championship was formally opened by the High Sheriff. He was accompanied by the Lady Mayor in full regalia. Following that piece of pomp the stage was turned over to the event chairman.

The marquee, in which were now corralled the club officials, stewards, rescue teams and of course competitors – well, most of them – was resonating from the increasing volume of human conversation. In an instant, however, it was hushed by the sound of tapping on a microphone. The obligatory ear-piercing feedback concentrated the audience's attention.

Not a particularly imposing character, the event chairman stepped forward to the front of the three-foot high stage. What he lacked in appearance he more than made up for in projection and diction. Standing, Richard reckoned, at around a portly 5'6", maybe a little taller, he sported a well-upholstered, well-fed belly.

His bushy sideboards and imposing, dark-framed bottle-ended spectacles focused everyone's attention. He was articulate; every syllable was clean and clear. Likely enough, he was involved in local drama. Even without a microphone he would have been heard on the pier-head. There were now probably a couple of hundred people, and it was time for the nitty-gritty. The dos and don'ts, and of course the finer aspects of the racing rules for the championship.

Richard was near the back of the crowd but he could hear him perfectly.

'Ladies and gentlemen, competitors...' You could have heard a pin drop.

The best part of an hour had passed, and Richard could see Dave Gilmour across from him, near the edge of the tent, getting very fidgety. He's in dire need of a drink, Richard thought, then felt a small pang of guilt. Finally, it was over. After a bite of lunch – cottage pie and salad – supplied free of charge, it was off to rig boats. To get changed into battle gear!

2: The Practice Race

The day provided perfect conditions; a summer breeze of hardly ten knots blew across a bay whose surface sparkled silver under a flock of dancing white sails. Not everyone participated in this practice race, yet it made a fine sight. The fleet waltzed jived and eventually addressed the starting line in formation and abreast, to open the event. The championship's first starting cannon fired in an explosion of blue smoke. The line was a little short and somewhat biased, but like *Team Satisfaction* the race officials were practising too.

Richard had always denied any suggestion of superstition. But he couldn't help being aware that to win the opening race of any championship was considered to be a bad omen. Where were the title contenders lying in the final furlongs of this race? Leading the bloody fleet.

Luckily Richard's denial was not to be put to the test that day. As they neared the finish, the much-fancied Mr. Simms and his crew for the championship, the colourful Julian Prendergast, nipped in ahead of them to take the week's first prize.

Julian had just made it home it time to take part in the event. He was again a UK resident. Clearing the finishing post, Richard leant over and enquired of Jonny: 'Where the bloody hell did they come from?'

'They stood out to the right-hand side of the course, out to starboard, which I recon must have been favoured this time around skipper.'

'Must remember that – but I wonder why it paid off quite so well?' Richard quietly pondered this quirk of the bay. He would use up a little more of the Archie knowledge bank when they got ashore. He had a feeling that Mr. MacAndrew would be there. He knew he would venture an opinion.

As they sailed quietly towards the little harbour breakwater in the late afternoon sun, they took the opportunity to convene their first debriefing session of the week. They were generally satisfied with their performance. Richard and Jonny were particularly pleased with the new sails; they especially enjoyed the crackling of the stiff new white Dacron sailcloth. They were also satisfied that Archie's advice, which had already proved useful, would continue to be dispensed as the week progressed.

Archie met them at the slipway with hearty congratulations – perhaps with an element of self-congratulation, or even relief.

Richard asked his question; five minutes later Archie was still explaining...

Their post-race routine of boat checks and tidying was interrupted. A mini melee had formed around them: competitors offering their congratulations, locals curious about how they (no direct comments about their northernness were mentioned...) mastered the conditions. It was a bit manic, but Richard was in his element.

As one well-dressed gent was in the process of introducing himself, Jonny cut across, to introduce him to another. He was a representative from their sail makers; the face behind that unexpected phone call, those many weeks ago. Somewhat awestruck, they were definitely not used to this type of attention, and their faffing and fidgeting gave them away.

A somewhat assertive type, tall, tanned, willowy in build and balding, the sailmaker took control. He was oblivious to the expansion of onlookers. He quizzed both Richard and Jonny; he asked them to elaborate on the settings they'd used out there; he questioned the rigging. Why had they set it up so tight? Then he moved on to mast positions, and so on. Up went the sails again!

There followed a personalised workshop: advice on how *his* sails should be set up, tips on fine tuning, etcetera. Questions and answers flowed. Glancing at his watch, Jonny realised that near on thirty minutes had flown by. He was mesmerised – he knew Richard was too– and he wasn't going to be a party-pooper. Glancing around, he too discovered that they had a new audience: he recognised John Simms. Then, almost as swiftly as it had started, the session ended.

Having finally put their mistress to bed Richard, with some hesitation, confessed to having learnt more in that last period than during the preceding three or four seasons. Jonny agreed. Their attention span was now exhausted.

An avalanche of voices summoned them to the marquee. They agreed – enough of that nautical stuff. Mid-afternoon was transforming itself into early evening. This was especially poignant for Jonny; he was, he remembered, a single bloke for the week. A quick change – they would shower later. It was indeed buzzing in there. Time to put one of their more serious theories to the test.

These boys totally believed in, and practiced their 'early bird theory' – this was the very occasion to roll it out; this was their big event. After many practical demonstrations over the years they had both convinced themselves that if you can seal a top-end result on the opening day of a regatta, your onshore status rises with equal buoyancy. Put another way, early rock star status gives early access to the babes!

So with a renewed sense of self-importance, misguided authority and false hope, they strutted expectantly into and through the marquee. Joining the multiple of ranks fronting the bar, once again they put theory into practice.

They were soon surrounded by well-wishers. There was Archie, and, well… no babes, just yet; the evening was yet young. They were full of confidence.

The detail of the practice race was soon written up on the jumbo-sized results board. The crush at the bar had eased. Many of the crowd wandered across the floor to read the listings. The boys were now better able to cast an eye around the gathering. For a moment Richard thought he had spied Samantha. No, he was mistaken. He also thought that wee Archie should be heading back to his Royal club. His monopolising of their company was starting to impinge on their – Richard's – magnetic pulling power.

As the results' audience thinned, Richard took the opportunity to drift over himself. Pint in hand, he drilled down through the detail. He considered taking a few early notes. Richard was a compulsive note taker... He immediately noted that Dave had retired from the race. But with a practice outing, that often happened, with some competitors opting out in favour of retuning. And then there were a few crews that he didn't recognise. An Irish team, for example, the O'Brien bothers, the only competitors from across the Irish Sea. He didn't recognise their names. Another duo, Ewan MacDonald and Alyson Firth, caught his eye. They were best of a strong contingent of nine Scottish crews.

Both of these teams, he noted, finished well up the fleet that day. There were also a few of the regular Dutch and French teams, but they were all well down the placings.

Then it clicked with him; the green boat, which finished just behind them today, was the O'Brien's; theirs was the boat which led round the first marker. He had no idea who those leading Scots were either, other than that they hailed from Helensburgh. Before returning to the bar he also checked on the performance of his club mates. They had both had a good day, recording a sixth and a tenth placing. Privately he was chuffed to have beaten them. Richard now had a fair idea where the main competition would come from. But he reminded himself that there are always surprises in sailboat racing. Homework completed, he sidled back towards the bar area.

His journey was aborted. He remembered his promise to call Uncle Jim. The club's public phone was queued. He nipped away from the tented village and across the esplanade to the nearest red box. Jim was delighted that his work had been appreciated. Richard didn't tell him about the smoke-impregnated VW. He kept wondering how the heck they were going to rid the van of the stale lingering of Archie's bloody pipe.

Following what was to become a daily prize giving, another fabulous night ensued. With a rockabilly band in full flow, the dance floor was swamped with revellers. Still mostly the club folks though; it always took a day or so for the fleet to get fully loosened up and suitably convivial.

Richard and Jonny, and of course the day's winners, John and the flamboyant Julian, remained the centre of attention. Fulfilling what they saw as an ambassadorial role, the boys attempted to communicate with all the females in attendance. They didn't differentiate between competitors or club hostesses. However and mindful of the challenge which lay ahead they were the absolute epitome of moderation, even slipping back to their quarters – unaccompanied – before the clock chimed midnight.

Conscious of the enormity of the task ahead, they eschewed nightcaps or midnight snacks. But as they tucked themselves in they were reminded of one early hurdle – Archie's aromatic presence.

'That flippin pipe is going to be with us all week,' Jonny complained.

'We should leave the windows wide open tomorrow.'

'Aye, and buy some of those air fresheners too.'

Richard mimicked Archie: 'Ay-ee. Good idea. Goodnight.' Richard claimed the last comment of the day.

3: Championship:
Day one, Race one (Monday)

'Now that was hard going.'

This was Richard's observation as they crossed the finishing line of the opening and progressively windy race.

'Agreed skipper, I feel as if I've been hit by a bus. I've got blisters on my fingers already,' said Jonny. Richard had never really heard Jonny complain before, but boy did he work up the last leg of that long course. They had been racing non-stop for nigh on two hours.

'Sure it was worth it, those three places we gained brought us up to fourth place. We could be a lot worse off,' was the skipper's sympathetic response. It was not really the start to the week that they wanted; beaten by their club mates Burton and Duffy. But it could have been worse. They were unfortunate to experience an early capsize, but the speed with which they recovered really saved the day.

They later discovered that John Simms was not so lucky. He too capsized. He was unfortunate to have damaged his tiller during the recovery. This had seriously impaired his ability to steer the boat efficiently. In the circumstances however, they both agreed that 10th place was very respectable in a fleet of this calibre.

Stating the obvious, Jonny said, 'He's clearly no slouch is our John. It was that green boat that won this race you know, Rich.' These and other observations were discussed as Richard steered *Satisfaction* homeward. All in all, they conceded that it had been an adequate opening to their campaign.

'Well that's those O'Brien brothers declaring their intentions for the championship', said Richard, feeling (secretly hoping, perhaps), that they had played their ace too early.

The offshore breeze had continued to build, so the boys' informal debriefing was aborted. Their sail back to the harbour into the teeth of was building into a near gale, became somewhat tricky. In fact, the closer they got to the shore the more difficult it was to control their bucking mistress. The gusts appeared to oscillate between Berry Head and Thatcher Rock, funnelling out into the bay with increasing venom. In one particularly nasty squall in which the wind seemed to empty vertically from the sky, all four of the leading boats were flattened.

That really was the last thing any of them needed. However, after some serious baling and a final few measured tacks, the harbour breakwater provided a welcome refuge. Once onto the slipway and into their parking space, the sails were quickly lowered and rolled away. After their clockwork inspection for wear and tear, their sailboat was carefully tucked away until tomorrow. Richard and Jonny headed straight for the washrooms. They needed to rid themselves of a covering layer of caked-on Torbay salt. Before they disappeared into the clubhouse, a stolen glance seaward revealed a scene of carnage. The extreme conditions were making life very difficult offshore. This applied not only to the fleet, but the event's support and rescue services. They heard later that the lifeboat and coastguard were put on standby.

'Oh boy,' Richard thought, 'there are going to be some tired limbs in here tonight...'

Crew	Boat Colour	Position	Points
O'Brien Brothers	Emerald green	First	¾
Burton & Duffy	Black	Second	2
Chisholme & Chisholme	Dark blue	Third	3
D'Arcy & Dubois	Grey	Fourth	4
Isherwood twins	Red &lime green	Fifth	5
Marsden & Staunton	Yellow/blue bottom	Sixth	6
Smith & O'Reilly	Maroon	Seventh	7
Hartley-Smyth & Hayes	White	Eighth	8
MacDonald & Firth	Pale Blue	Ninth	9
Simms & Prendergast	White	Tenth	10

Positions after Race One

Giving the marquee catering an early miss, the boys treated themselves to well-deserved Wimpy & chips at an outlet they'd noticed previously down along the esplanade. Their gourmet needs satisfied, they wound their way back to the club. Jonny took the opportunity to ring Penny from the telephone box.

'Catch you later mate,' he said to Richard.

Richard dodged the traffic and carried on to the marquee. An even more deserved Watneys was consumed. The marquee was filling up and the atmosphere building. He bumped into a fairly incoherent Dave Gilmore. Jeez, thought Richard, he looks as if he hit the drink after he hit the beach.

'What now?' he asked himself. But before he could speak Dave had wrapped himself around his shoulder.

'Ricky my boy! Come 'ere – what you suppin?'

Boy, he was really drowning his sorrows. Retired from the practice race yesterday, he said, because he was bored. That was code for a severe hangover. But today he had left the leading pack when his rudder snapped off in one of those furious squalls. And Richard thought *his* title chase got off to a slow-ish start!

Harnessing his street savvy, Richard sympathetically extracted Dave from the glare of the main bar. He guided him off into a siding at the rear of the marquee; out of harm's way, but importantly very much away from public view. In the seclusion of the siding Richard hoped that he would emerge from a drunken sleep and quietly drift back to his lodgings. He had great respect for this guy. It disturbed him, knowing that he was witnessing an early demise.

No sooner had he dealt with Dave boy than Michael arrived. Wow, was he pissed off; ahead of him he had the unenviable task of removing Dave, back to the loving arms of their landlady. Methinks those two guys are maybe not in just the right frame of mind to defend their title, predicted Richard. Boy, was he about to get that prediction wrong …

It was becoming one of those 'getting to know you' nights. Next up were the O'Brien's. Eoin and Fergal were born in County Wicklow but lived in the north of Ireland. They sailed, he discovered, out of a Strangford Lough club. By the sound of it, it was a magical place to do your yachting. Already Richard was captivated by the O'Brien's: the brogue, their way with words, their storytelling.

Jonny appeared, then two of the Scottish folk, Ewan MacDonald and his crew, Alison Firth. There were a few others; he didn't get their names.

'Fit looking girl, eh? I think she likes me,' Jonny whispered to Richard. Jonny's remark had caught him off-guard. His mate wasn't prone to such deliberate comment; a one man women was the Jonny boy. He though no more of it, but darted a glance back at his mate...

A P.E. teacher, they learned later. She played top-level hockey over the winter, then sailed and biked in the summer. She was not, however, looking and lusting at Jonny, as he was destined to discover. No, it seemed that Fergal was the one in her sights. Of this, the young O'Brien was totally unaware. Jonny passed the observation on to his skipper, and Richard agreed.

'Where you seriously going to make a move on her?' he queried. Jonny didn't answer he arose and wandered off. It provoked Richard to think of a certain Samantha. The mystery of her continuing absence was beginning to nirk him. He was unsettled, as indeed Jonny appeared to be. *Nerves, yeah, its nerves. Both of us are wound up like springs.*

He tried to focus on the sailing. He was curious about a guy with a hyphenated name who got eighth place earlier; a bit of a public school entry. Hartley-Smyth...? He enquired of Herbie Martin, crew for Darren Brett.

'Oh, that's her over there.' Herbie gestured, pint in hand.

*Her?!*Bloody hell, thought Richard. Still, he might as well finish what he started. Fresh pint in hand, he plunged into the growing crowd, stalking his target …

'Hi there, I'm Richard D'Arcy. That was a fantastic sail today. Did you manage okay out there?' A somewhat derogatory opener, and it occurred to him, too late, that he was being a patronising little git. Well, at least he didn't call her 'little lady'. He couldn't help thinking of his equally stupid opening remarks to Samantha on their initial meeting.

'Yes we did Richard, thanks for asking, but when you've got a gorilla like Robin here hanging over the side, all you do is steer the boat in the right general direction. By the way I'm Hayley. You're one of the favourites I believe; you're off to a great start – 4th today?'

'Yes.' Richard tried to retrieve his assertiveness. 'We're pleased with that, but I understand it's going to go light and shifty tomorrow.'

He was about engage in further aquatic tittle-tattle when she grabbed his arm.

'Come on, put your pint down and dance with me, I love this song...'

Four dances later they were they were making their way back at the bar to join Jonny.

Behind your posh name, you're a bit of a down-to-earth gal, he concluded silently. And boy can you dance – maybe not my style; but dance nevertheless.

He was within touching distance of the bar when Alison unhitched Hayley's hand and ushered him back to the floor for the next set. KC & The Sunshine Band brought out his best dance moves, and his worst. They sang along: *'That's the way, ah ha...'*

Then he sobered himself. He'd better watch himself or he'd be knackered tomorrow. Still, no point in wasting opportunities. Never know where they might lead. Richard was ever the opportunist. It was then, as he was swinging Alison round – or she was swinging him – that he saw her; he definitely saw her! The set ended, and

Richard led Alison, with some purpose, back to her table. He excused himself and went off on safari.

Samantha was in this tent, and damn it, he would find her if it killed him. Actually his trek was short-lived. As he spun away from Alison's table he caught Michael Murphy on the elbow, spilling his Coke. Michael refused a replacement. Richard suspected that he was so pissed off with Dave's behaviour earlier, he had reckoned at least one of them needed to be alert, if not sober, for tomorrow. Then, over Michael's left shoulder he saw Jonny holding up the bar with ... Samantha.

It was happening again; as he closed in on them, his stomach was churning. His mouth was dry, his nerves tingled.

Before he could utter a word, Jonny said: 'Hey mate, look who I found.' Samantha reached out her hand.

'It's been a long time, Richard. Or is it Ricky? How have you been?' Samantha spoke almost in a whisper. Her voice was barely audible against the background of music and bar noise. Richard, however, caught every word, every sentence, every syllable. Reaching out his arm, his fingertips touched hers. It happened again; like a static shock. Almost without hesitation Richard, his fingers now under-locking hers, glided closer. On his final approach she turned ever so slightly. Instead of a 'cheek-to-cheek' they actually kissed, quickly and softly. It was a juvenile kiss, innocent. But it confirmed, if confirmation were needed, that he had been right all along.

With their eyes locked, conversation had stalled. Jonny broke the deadlock.

'Listen comrades, I'm feeling a bit shattered – going to turn in early, okay?'

Instinctively, Richard realised something wasn't right. He turned his attention momentarily away from Samantha.

'What's up? Mate, the night is young,' he said to Jonny.

'No, no I'm okay, just dog tired. Anyway, someone's got to be fit tomorrow.' He turned away.

'Jonny...?' A somewhat bemused Richard tried again.

'Look, just leave it. And don't waken me, okay?' There was more than tiredness in his voice.

Richard turned back to Samantha, now perched statuesque on a barstool. She didn't need a spotlight to emphasise her presence; she radiated.

'I'm sorry about that, he's not himself. Hope he's not coming down with something.'

'Yes he did seem a bit glum when I met him – I suspect its girl problems.'

'It seems a long time since I fell out of that clubhouse door.' Richard attempted to manoeuvre the conversation away from Jonny and over to him, hopefully to them.

'Oh, that was so funny. Did you really not hurt yourself? Suppose you were being a typical hard man?'

'Hurt? As soon as I was out of sight I damned near collapsed. I really thought I'd broken my ankle – I blame it entirely on you.'

'On me? Why?'

'Well, having been such a total tongue-tied twit that morning you literally threw me off-balance when you called after me. You really did.' He looked at her and frowned. 'I mean, why would you, why would *anyone* want to catch up with an ass like me again after...'

She stopped him; her first and second finger touched his mouth.

'Maybe I just like challenges. Fancy a dance? And by the way sailor, don't be tempted to enter the Devon county dance competition.'

He was an easy target. He was putty in her hands.

'Oh my God, you pair were watching me out there – was it that bad?' He was grateful for dimmed lighting; it concealed his blushes.

'Umm … yes, frankly; but you weren't just as bad as those girls, especially Hayley.'

'Yeah, she was a bit mad. I'll do better this time, I promise.'

She was leading him. They entered the dance floor into the frenzy that was the 'Hippy Hippy Shake'. The DJ, almost as if had been pre-planned, mellowed the mood and wound up the volume on the Mindbenders: 'A Groovy Kind of Love'.

Lucky break, Richard thought. Not too many slow sets are played anymore. And, like a seasoned professional, he politely extended his left arm around her waist as she placed her hand on his shoulder. A little nervously, their free hands joined. Midway into the dance, she released his hand, placing hers on his other shoulder. Then it slipped around his neck to clasp her other hand. Gently his forehead was pulled against hers. Richard was now holding her waist with both hands, thinking: should I?

As he exerted some pressure, Samantha willingly, and in time with the music, moved closer. Her head was now against his right cheek. Her fine blond hair tickled his closed eyelids. He could feel her firm breasts against his chest. He wondered if she in turn could sense his arousal. His heart raced. They didn't notice the song ending, or the next dance beginning. Their embrace remained locked. Mini Riperton preceded Joe Cocker who in turn extended their much-anticipated moment of magic with 'You Are So Beautiful'; they were lost in their private embrace.

Suddenly the tempo went upbeat. Elvis had entered the building. In a flash he was back into his 'dance' routine. She laughed so hard that she ended up looking as idiotic as him. Exiting the floor, and indeed the marquee, they found favour in the member's bar. The music was muffled and in secluded alcove they chatted on oblivious, happy in each other's company.

Suddenly she jumped up from the table.

'Richard I'd love to stay, but I've promised to get Daddy home by 12:30 – he's a bit lost without Mum these days.'

'Yes, I was so sorry to hear – Jonny told me.' Richard was somewhat flustered.

'Look,' she said. 'I'm on duty at the hospital this week, bad timing eh? But I will be back down during the week. We can talk a bit more.'

She gave him a peck on the cheek, light but somehow sensual.

'Yes, yes of course,' he said, stumbling after her. But she was gone. Only her perfume lingered, and it dawned on him that that was all he had – a scent. No name, address, or phone number. However, safe in the knowledge that she would indeed be back, such things seemed trivial. Wandering back to the VW, Richard hadn't a care in the world; he didn't even notice the rain.

'Dreams,' he told himself, 'can and do come true'.

4: Championship:
Day Two (Tuesday)

Tuesday dawned grey. Jonny had cooked breakfast again – his student training continued to impress – but he was quiet, sullen.

'Hey mate, want to talk about it?' Richard opened proceedings.

'Na, just leave it Rich, just leave it; we'll talk later.' And with that he passed Richard his fry, and wandered off.

'Fuck me that's my happy morning bubble well and truly burst,' Richard mumbled. 'This is some way to go into battle ...'

He stepped out of the VW. The wet grass tickled his bare feet. He gestured good morning to the girls in the tent opposite, had a private snigger. It wasn't enough to brighten his deflated morning though. Hands in pockets, feet in flip-flops, he strolled down to the dinghy park, but today, without the usual panache. Shoulders hunched and head bowed, Richard kicked at the grass as he was overtaken by the Scots.

'Bit o' a dreich yin today Ricky,' announced a boisterous Ewan MacDonald.

'Dreich? What the hell is dreich?'

'This, Richard,' explained Alison, 'is Ewan's Scottish weather forecast – grey, grey and wet, wet, wet. A bit like you and Jonny this morning.'

'You two have a lover's tiff?' said Ewan.

'Oh, I'm not sure …Think it might be women trouble.'

'Oh dear, know exactly how he feels then.' Ewan's quip was rewarded with a dead arm inflicted by the grinning Alison. Richard instinctively found his sense of humour, stepping swiftly out of range, his arm raised in surrender.

'Now now, girl – I don't necessarily agree...'

'Coward,' she joked. As their ways parted Richard wondered, just as he and Jonny had wondered yesterday: Are they a couple?

The start of their second outing was delayed for two hours. This was to allow any available breeze to fill in. One o'clock was the deadline. This postponement was made official by the hoisting of a red and white pennant to fly – hang – from the yardarm on the seaward side of the clubhouse.

It was a blessing, but that was nothing to do with the weather. It provided Richard with time to think through why Jonny's mood had changed so dramatically. He caught up with Jonny some ten minutes later.

He was slouched against the harbour wall, flicking pebbles. Easing him shoreward and into the marquee, Richard bought him a coffee. Sip by sip he prized out of him what was weighing so heavily. Sure enough, he and Penny had had a falling out – their first proper one. He was hundreds of miles away and she was stuck at home on her own. Richard sort of thought that she and her mother weren't getting on. Of course Jonny was down on the English Riviera having, as she called it, the time of his life... He also suspected it was the time of the month. He didn't, for once, say anything. Rightly or wrongly he urged, persuaded, bullied Jonny to ring her and apologise; what for, he had no idea. If he was honest, he cared little. It was worth anything to get *his* Jonny back. Jonny eventually agreed. It had taken a while, but he seemed to be back – Halleluiah!

The wind, what there was of it, had filled in. It was noon. The pennant fluttered. Soon it was lowered. This signalled the re-commencement of activities. The clubhouse was evacuated and the fleet were off to the races. It was to be a three o'clock start– Halleluiah! again.

The wind had more or less swung through the compass and settled into the southeast. It was blowing onshore, so the sail out to the starting area was relatively short compared to yesterday. The boys were one of the first crews to arrive in the race area.

They spent the extra time working out the idiosyncrasies of the first leg of what would be another nine-mile course. From the starting line to the first mark would be one nautical mile.

In these conditions it would be slow going and mentally gruelling. Richard's thoughts briefly turned to poor old Dave – but no sympathy was offered. This was serious competition. The major event on the calendar; there for the winning. If he chose to manufacture hurdles and hangovers well, that was his problem. He should know better – after all, he was the defending champion. Richard was pumped up!

It wasn't so much of an high decibel crack but a low resolution booming sound. A sword of pale grey smoke was the visible signal that they were away first time. The smoke drifted downwind over the big anchored starting boat and officials onboard were quietly relieved to see the fleet away without incident.

'Surely John Simms and Julian were premature; no? Guess they got away with it,' Said Jonny quietly. He wished that Richard could get out of the starting lines the way they always seemed to. As they homed in on the first mark they contented themselves that they were within the leading bunch. Jonny continued to communicate information to his skipper.

'The green boat is again well placed, as is Simms, and... bugger me, I do not believe what I'm seeing. It's dark hull leading; it couldn't be. Na, its dark blue... or is it?' Jonny eyes refocused in deeper disbelief: the colour of the leading hull was certainly dark, but not as he thought, blue. It was brown; mahogany – and in it were Dave and Michael!

'The man's not human,' said Richard. 'After the state he was in last night, too.'

They rounded fifth behind a dark blue boat which eagle-eyed Jonny realised was local – he could just make out the host club's name written onto its stern. They just beat us yesterday, he realised.

'They're doing some mouthing, those guys,' said Richard. 'Aggressive to the point of being nasty.' He instinctively instructed himself: *Give them a wide berth ...*

As the race wore on the conditions never really settled down. And the instability of the wind encouraged much place-changing throughout the fleet. Except for Dave and Michael ... They had opened up a commanding lead of approximately ten boat-lengths on the second-placed team of MacDonald and Firth. John and Julian were third, fractionally ahead of the green boat.

'So much for sailmakers' tips Jonny – we're back to buts again.'

As they were late ashore, the customary after-race pint was given up in favour of an invigorating shower. Ewan's 'dreich' prediction had indeed materialised, and the competitors resembled drowned rats as they scurried back to shore.

Race 2	Helm & crew	Race 1	Accumulated points
1st	Gilmore & Murphy	Ret'd	83¾ points
2n	MacDonald & Firth	9th	11 points
3rd	Simms & Prendergast	10th	13 points
4th	O'Brien brothers	1st	4¾ points
5th	Marsden & Staunton	6th	11 points
6th	Isherwood twins	5th	11 points
7th	Smith & O'Reilly	7th	14 points
8th	**D'Arcy & Dubois**	4th	12 points
9th	Burton & Duffy	2nd	11 points
10th	Brett & Martin	27th	37 points

Results for Race Two

Dried, powdered and changed, a reinvigorated Richard once again extracted the relevant information from the official results board. He copied it to his personal log book, charting the detail of Race Two and noting the accumulated scores before exiting the village, back to the relative comfort of the living quarters to cogitate.

Regardless of the day's triumph, Dave and Michael's cumulative points score still looked disastrous. John and Julian's weren't looking too clever either, very much like themselves. But Richard and Jonny were consoled in the knowledge that these were early days. Assuming that every race was run, each competitor in the championship would discard their worst result. So in no way could any of them be regarded as beaten dockets, not yet. Equally, although the Irish team were currently way out in front, a couple of mediocre finishes would quickly reel them back in; early days indeed, a soldierly Richard reminded himself. He sipped a hot chocolate. Then, looking out over a damp campsite while Radio One rattled out its late afternoon music with Alan Freeman, he decided it was time to consider the evening's social strategy... Jonny had already given over his early evening schedule to the telephone. He was surely apprising Penny of his gruelling day at the races.

Back at the village and dressed accordingly, the anticipation of his rendezvous easily erased the memory of their erratic form afloat. His principal thought was the expansion of the embryonic relationship with his current reason for living, the mysterious Samantha.

'Pint of Watneys Red please, mate,' he asked the young bartender.

'I'll get that.' Over his shoulder, he saw that Michael Murphy had sidled up to the bar.

'Cheers, thanks mate.'

It was still early and they grabbed a quite booth in an empty corner of the club lounge.

'Quiet before the storm eh?' said Michael.

'Talking of storms ... You guys were on fire out there today – how the bloody hell does he recover like that?' Richard frowned and continued. 'I mean, he couldn't even bite his finger last night.'

'Tell me about it!' Michael, cupping his pint with both hands, leaned across the table. There was a look of serious intent on his face. His lips tightened and his brown eyes were fixed.

'You know Rich, I have just about had it up to here with the wee shite.'

Suddenly his whole demeanour had become somewhat menacing. Although he wouldn't have carried himself as tall as Jonny he was nevertheless a big lad. Richard somehow felt a little intimidated. He too adopted an upright posture, sitting back defensively into the upholstery.

'I appreciate your predicament,' he said, mustering as much sympathy as he could. He spoke in a soft tone. He tried hard to present a calming, listening face. His stare, however, kept focusing on Michael's latest facial accessory, a droopy handlebar moustache. It just seemed to emphasise his sullen expression. And it was very ginger. Taking a deep breath, Richard continued:

'He does look like a guy who's got problems.'

He was intrigued now. His curiosity had taken over and he was fuelling the fire. He leaned over the table himself, gulped some beer, and waited...

'Business going sour. Marriage even sourer. And the drinking, well it's near enough out of control.' Michael, having got that off his chest, did appear calmer, but Richard realised that a treasure chest had started to open.

'What came first?'

'That's a very good question.' Michael paused for a moment. 'Probably the whole marriage thing: the shotgun wedding I suppose? The baby was followed by the realisation that he and Sal had nothing in common. That's how I saw it anyway. Then she had it off with another bloke. Apparently she blurted this out in the middle of yet another blazing row. Big fight down the pub! Dave broke the guy's nose and jaw.' Information flowed from Michael like an ebb tide. 'Then she moved back to the mother complete with child; don't need to tell you the rest.'

Michael sat upright; he pressed back into the padding of the alcove upholstery. He gulped back half of his pint. The ebb tide had, it seemed, slackened.

'Flippin 'eck, never knew or suspected a thing; thought he just liked his booze.'

Richard was not quite ready to let it go. He probed further.

'What sort of business does he have?'

One side of his brain was telling him to extract himself while the other, the inquisitive side, was dragging him in deeper. Conversation, however, remained on hold as they supped the remaining life out of their respective pints.

'Another lager Mike?'

His visit to the bar allowed more of the sting to dissipate from Michael – big Mike had just needed someone to open up to, someone with whom he could allow his dam of frustration to burst.

Richard now worried that Michael would dry up completely. The lounge was starting to fill up. He hurried back to the booth...

'There you go mate.' He handed over a fresh pint. 'So what's Dave's business again?' He chose his words carefully, phrasing the question in such a way as to encourage Michael to relight the flame. There was a short pause.

'Yeah...he's in the marine trade, he owns a small boat yard and repair facility – could be a real goldmine.' Richard was suddenly aware that his friend had gifted him with perhaps too much detail; nevertheless he persevered.

'Gold mine?'

'Yes, Dave is a real craftsman and just knows boats inside-out, but he's taken his eye off the ball. He's not watching out for his regular clientele. He rarely chases up new work – sometimes he doesn't even show up at the yard!'

Richard was entranced. Michael continued:

'I mean... I know what it's like. If I treated my customers the way he's treating his, my old man's furniture shop wouldn't keep the shutters up too long. The trouble with Dave is, he's stubborn. He won't be told. Of course with all the current background noise, he's just not hearing anyone. Yes Ricky, it's a problem. A problem that I've no answer for – simple as that!'

Michael leaned over, his voice dropping another octave.

'Look mate— I've said far too much. I really appreciated your time and ear, but ask that you keep all this to yourself, if you don't mind. It's really important than no-one, and mean NO-one, hears about this – I haven't told Dave yet that I'm parting company with him at the end of this event.'

Richard looked directly at Michael and said: 'You have my word on that.' And he meant it.

'Hey, let's go chase the talent in the big tent,' said Michael, giving Richard an appreciative slap on the back. They were off towards the marquee. It was wall-to-wall people in there, but with a professional, done-it-all-before swagger, big Michael worked his way up to the front, gently moving people aside.

As they arrived at the podium Mike joined Dave to collect their day's winnings from the commodore. Following behind, this was the closest Richard had come to the main prizes this week. It was also his first close encounter with the commodore.

He was a lean old bloke, about 5'6", silver-grey hair, central parting combed back from a high-ish forehead. He sported a fine RAF-style moustache and of course wore the obligatory blue reefer and grey flannel trousers. He mumbled a few words to the gathering. Richard didn't really catch what he said, and wondered idly why these guys didn't use the microphones provided. He was irritated by little things like that.

His task completed, the commodore made his way carefully from the podium. Negotiating the crowd that milled around the stage, he stopped beside Richard.

'Oh, you must be young D'Arcy – I've heard good reports. Respectable result today, no?' Somewhat surprised, Richard replied hastily:

'Yes, but we'll need to do much, much better, tomorrow, but thank you for that.'

'Ah, patience young man, patience,' and with that he melted into the crowd.

What a lovely man, thought Richard. Obviously knew exactly what was what. He scanned the faces in hope of sighting the mysterious Samantha. If she hadn't intended meeting again, why didn't she just tell him so last night? Dark thoughts began to form in his mind. With the elation of early evening more or less evaporated along with his expectations, he wondered if he should find Michael and give him a taste of his own medicine. It was his turn to have a good moan.

Stop it Richard. Now you're being nasty. He tried to ignore the feeling of frustration. *She's obviously not coming. Wasted too much bloody time on one babe – mind, she was rather delicious and beautiful ...*

Stroking his chin, he mumbled aloud: 'So let me see. What's on offer this evening?' First into his sights was the bubbly and slightly scary Miss Harley-Smyth. He bought her a drink; she, like him, preferred Bacardi. They had a few dances. He reckoned he was in there, but then realised that he wasn't really that interested... The same scenario played out for Richard during the rest of the evening.

He resorted to alcohol, inwardly complaining, feeling more and more sorry for himself. *That flaming Samantha, she is really messin' with my head. What's happening to me?* Then, the final straw: the DJ struck up another set with Sandy Shaw's 'Girl Don't Come!'

'You couldn't make it up,' he grunted. He signalled for a refill. Instead of Michael rescuing his helmsman, it would be Jonny's turn tonight...

Working his way out of an alcoholic slumber, the waft of breakfast did not immediately gel with Richard's digestive system. But the daily trek to the campsite 'facilities' and a good splashing of cold water brought him to his senses. No hangover, he noted with some surprise; at the same time realising a vague feeling of guilt about his ongoing lack of culinary contribution. This morning's retribution was the washing up.

His unexpected bout of domesticity turned somewhat to embarrassment when Jonny started to spill the beans on the previous night's performance. Oops. We won't go down that road again, he promised himself.

More embarrassment was to come. Retracing his footsteps from campsite to marquee, he could not but notice the 'splats' along the route – silent witness to the excesses of the night before, and the absence of a hangover.

5: Championship:
Day Three (Wednesday)

Another day had dawned in the quest for aquatic stardom. This day, however, was bright and dry. The forecast posted on the official championship notice board told of a steady Force 2 from the south, perhaps increasing to Force 4 later.

'Another exciting day at the races, Rich?' Jonny's tongue was firmly in his cheek.

'Yeah great, another gift of a day for the lightweights – bet this'll wipe the smile off Dave and Michael's faces.' He remarked with a degree of sarcasm that they had an all up weight of thirty-one stone plus. He and Jonny were no lightweights either, but were certainly not in that league.

The starting area was a bit manic for this, the third race of the series. As the countdown for the start began, the boys were instantly aware of something more than the normal pre-race jostling. The close-quarters jousting of one particularly hostile crew was forcing *Satisfaction* perilously close to the starting line, and too soon …

'Skipper, we're going to be early, far too early!' warned Jonny.

'I know I know, but these fuckers beside us have me boxed in. They're forcing us forward. I can't allow them to hit us – if they do we're disqualified. I've dropped my guard. We're in a scary place right now!' An air of panic was evident in Richard's voice. His only option was to up the aggression stakes – and shout.

'WHAT THE FUCK ARE YOU TRYING TO DO?' he hollered at the aggressors. 'BEAR AWAY, BEAR AWAY! SAIL FOR THE STARTING LINE YOU STUPIT IDIOTS!!'

But to no avail. With seven seconds left on the clock they were now significantly early: They were on the course side of the starting line. *Satisfaction* will clearly be premature. Richard had no way of reversing her back to re-start. They were in trouble, big trouble!

'Oh no, oh no. I'm screwed,' said Richard, half to himself.

Grey hull or not, Jonny also knew that even the most short-sighted and colour blind official would be able to identify them. Already he too was scanning, looking for an exit. No route existed. He and his skipper resigned themselves to their fate... Three. Two. One …

BANG! Then, several seconds later, a second cannon had fired – more clouds of dissipating smoke. More signal flags flew from the anchored starting boat. Jonny was about to relay this unwanted information but his skipper spoke first. It was in a dejected tone.

'Yep, that's the recall gun for us, Jonny – sorry mate, I just didn't see those fuckers early enough.' Richard was beside himself with disappointment and frustration at his own carelessness. But also boiling up was rage. He slapped his hand hard on the deck. The stinging pain didn't help matters. The seconds ticked by, probably ten or fifteen, though it felt like an eternity. As they navigated back towards the starting area, and out around the starting boat, the air suddenly resonated. A shock wave precipitated another cannon, the third. This time they were enveloped within the smoke cloud. Startled, but it was the skipper who declared; 'Bloody hell, the luck of the Irish,' Richard shouted. His deflation had turned to elation, a mixture of joy and disbelief. Jonny looked somewhat bewildered. 'Umm, we're not Irish, Richard.'

'We are today mate.' He still couldn't believe their luck. The third cannon he had explained to Jonny, signalled to the competitors a general recall; the start was void, and the whole fleet – all eighty-three boats – were back to square one. Confirmation flags fluttered in the warm breeze. It was a joyous sight for Richard.

'For a general recall to occur,' Richard explained to Jonny, 'either the race officials' view of the fleet was completely obscured or too many competitors, too many to identify, were also premature with their run into the start.' The sermon continued: 'So treat that as your great escape, and our lucky omen!'

'Rich,' Jonny enquired, 'who were those guys anyway?'

'Oh, who else? Locals – remember the dark blue boat yesterday? No doubt out to take a big scalp so they can boast to their club mates for months afterwards.' Richard had anger lodged in his throat. For a few moments, silence reigned. Then his anger resurfaced.

'Worst of all mate, I had picked them out as trouble yesterday – remember? To be honest Jonny, I'm more cross with myself. I mean it was a schoolboy error – aaargh!' He slapped the deck again. Then suddenly, as they milled around awaiting the re-start sequence, there was the same boat, just ahead... Richard blew. He couldn't contain himself.

'HEY YOU. ASSHOLE!' Richard bellowed. They both turned.

'You ever, EVER, try that stunt again and I swear I'll put you and your precious little boat so far over the next start you'll not recover for the rest of the week – DICK-HEADS!!!' Anger expunged, in stony silence and under the gaze of a lock-jawed audience, they tacked away. The boys never encountered them again on a starting line. Jonny just looked at Richard, shook his bowed head, and refocused. His eyes were locked on the starting boat and its crew of officials.. He was readied for the new sequence of starting signals.

'Feeling a bit better now are we, skipper?'

The cannon duly performed its functions; loud and visible. They were away clean.

'Nice one skipper.'

And indeed it was. In fact it was so good that it was they who led the fleet round the first mark. They were just ahead of their club mates, Owen and Graham. John and Julian rounded third and then it was Dave and Michael, who seemed to have got themselves into a bit of a personal dual with the O'Brien's.

Spinnaker set, they started to discuss their options. To say that they were rather pleased to actually lead a fleet again would have been an understatement. It became a difficult day though. Again, it featured much place-changing. Too much place-changing in fact. What had started out as a comfortable lead eventually evaporated into a second place. Messer's Gilmore and Murphy appeared to have picked up a personalised breeze; again, it was out to the right side of the course.

They shaved across *Satisfaction's* bow to steal the result. Dave and Mike had been accelerated from fourth to first place, in one move – Richard was not impressed in the slightest, friend or no friend.

'Bugger...' An exasperated Jonny could not contain his frustration.

'Am I ever going to win a race again? This better not be a bad omen.' The frustration was evident in Richard's voice.

'Mind, the Irish have had an even worse day.' Jonny attempted to lift the despair that seemed to have engulfed the boat. He was grasping at straws. Richard remained crestfallen. He mumbled, 'So near...'

Jonny said:

'Well, otherwise well sailed, skipper. It's still a good result, eh?'
Richard finally smiled. It was thin but he nodded in acknowledgement.

'Yeah, of course it'll do our points tally no harm at all. But a wee bit of silverware would have been nice.' Richard was less successful than Jonny at putting a brave face on it.

'It'll come, skipper, it'll come, just calm yourself. At least we beat Alan and Paddy'

Race 3	Helm & crew	Race 1	Race 2	Accumulated points	Current placing
1st	Gilmore & Murphy	Ret'd	1st	84½	N/A
2^{n}	**D'Arcy & Dubois**	4th	8th	14	Joint lead
3rd	Burton & Duffy	2nd	9th	14	Joint lead
4th	Isherwood twins	5th	6th	15	Equal forth
5th	Marsden & Staunton	6th	5th	16	fifth
6th	Simms & Prendergast	10th	3rd	19	Equal sixth
7th	Smith & O'Reilly	7th	7th	21	Eighth
8th	MacDonald & Firth	9th	2nd	19	Equal sixth
9th	Hartley-Smyth & Lewis	8th	50th	67	N/A
10th	O'Brien Brothers	1st	4th	14¾	Third

Results after Race 3

A now upbeat Richard was browsing the results and updating his analysis – his evening ritual. They now held the joint lead in the championship. Realising that it was with his club mates had cheered him up no end. He allowed himself a wry grin at place number 50.

157

Shame, he thought ... Then he felt a pang of guilt, a small pang. Maybe he *had* been a bit over the top out there; best apologise he thought.

Without warning there came a loud thud. Vision darkened and blurred. He found himself gasping for breath, his legs lifted from the marquee floor. His mouth and nose were pinned hard against something solid – the notice board, he thought. He wriggled furiously. He twisted his torso. A gripping hand was biting into the nape of his neck; his arms were free but flailing. After what seemed like an eternity, he managed to roll around, wiping his nose, it occurred to him, against the results of the lower half of the fleet. He grasped his aggressor's wrist and forced the hand away, but it was on his throat again before he could take a full breath. He fought hard. Once again, he loosened the fingers. This allowed for a moment's sucking of much-needed oxygen, and he tried to regain his bearings. Then it started.

'CHAPPY, DON'T you EVER, ever, EVER speak to me like that again! Just who do you think you are coming down here you pumped-up little shit? Richard's world had been spun into slow motion. He sucked in great gulps of air, his head spinning. Pictures of dark blue boats flashed by... He had truly been caught off-guard.

Trying to reason his senses he registered, almost subconsciously, that one doesn't expect this kind of loutish behaviour in yachting circles. The penny had dropped. The posh one! The starting line incident! He continued to fight and wriggle like a terrier.

158

Strange thoughts entered his head: *you can forget your apology mate*; then, *how the fuck am I going to get this bean-pole off me…?* The scuffle continued. Whatever was being said, Richard wasn't listening. The guy had completely lost the plot. Whilst no longer able to decipher his aggressor's diction, he fully understood his intent. It had been a long time since Richard had been involved in a bar-room brawl. But he remembered the escape rules...

His street savvy had finally broken the surface. He had managed to wriggle free and now it was him in the driving seat. Grasping both of his assailant's flailing arms, he wrestled him into a nearby chair between the side of the stage, and the results board at the top end of the big tent. They were eyeball-to-eyeball again, but Richard had gained the upper hand. Their noses almost touching, he made a suggestion.

'Grow up and quit making an ass of yourself, tallboy! What exactly is your problem?'

With the tempest momentarily abated, young D'Arcy freed his grip and turned away, but bloody hell, didn't the tallboy, like a jack-in-the-box, come straight back at him! This time, however, his crewman, his little brother, and a couple of club people – including the commodore – intercepted him. He was bundled away through an opening in the canvas. His brother had peeled off and Richard, although pale and shaken, was fully prepared for the second round. The guy raised both his palms, and apologised for his brother's aggression.

'I'm really sorry friend; never seen Hilary so agitated and upset.' After a pause Richard, quelling his natural instinct for an inappropriate wise-crack, quietly replied between coughs:

'Look — no harm done — mate. And — I'm Richard — by the way.'

'Henry. Henry Chisholme.' Richard replied: 'I think I too should apologise for my language out there today.' A two-way olive-branching session seemed appropriate. They both smiled. Richard sat down, still coughing, rubbing his neck. A combination of sunburn and fingernails was causing him a degree of irritation.

'Accepted,' replied an evidently relieved Henry. They shook hands at the edge of the dance floor while righting a few of the scattered chairs, then tentatively they strolled across and out of the marquee into the clubhouse. He bought Richard a much-needed cold pint before heading back to the battlefield, or perhaps it was now a counselling chamber. Neither the brothers nor the (presumably embarrassed) commodore were seen for the rest of the evening. The event chairman, who personally apologised to Richard on behalf of the club, did the evening prize giving.

Richard had never seen such big smile before, and the silly git even winked at him as his day's winnings were collected.

'Sometimes, Dave Gilmore, I really hate you.' He was sure Jonny was thinking the same. The excitement of Richard's late afternoon skirmish was trumped by Jonny's news, imparted with some excitement back at the van: the lovely Penny, it seemed, was arranging to pay them a royal visit after all. She would arrive tomorrow. Great, thought Richard, with just a tinge of inward sarcasm. That'll be me into the tent then. Perhaps he was letting the pressure get to him. He wasn't normally that fussed.

'What a day' Richard sighed aloud. Jonny was already asleep.

And with that, day three was signed off.

6: Championship:
Day Four (Thursday)

'Can't believe it's Thursday. Where has the week gone?' said Jonny.
He looked sideways at Richard, continuing, '... and I can't believe
that dickhead Chisholme – wonder if he'll show his face today.
What's his problem Rich? Pity I hadn't been around — I'd have
launched him into Torbay.'

'Yeah, Jonny boy. Always in the wrong place at the right time.'

'OK, but why was he so aggressive Rich?'

'Well it's like this, Jonny my boy.' Richard was suddenly the
Wise Old Man of the Sea. 'If you were blessed with a Christian
name like Hilary, would you not be a bit reactionary? I mean,
Hilary? Do you know any guys called Hilary? Bet he took some
stick in the playground. Perhaps Johnny Cash will write a song for
him – my name is ...'

He was in top form. It was his way of rinsing the whole incident from his head. Jonny was horrified. He just looked at Richard, his mouth ajar.

'I *do not* believe the things you come off with at times Ricky – you really are full of it. I suppose you've never heard of the 5th century Pope Hilary, or Hilary of Chichester...? Feeling somewhat superior, he continued: 'And then there was the explorer. No, he was Edmond. Hil...'

Richard stopped him.

'Okay, okay, you've made your point. And by the way, I've told you before – don't call me Ricky.'

'Oohhhhh. Still Mr Aggressive are we?'

They finished breakfast – Richard's offering – washed up and made their way to the dinghy park.

'What do you think Penny's first comment will be when she steps into the VW?'

Richard was attempting to wind Jonny up again. They were now standing in front of the official championship notice board. A check on the weather forecast indicated a perfect day for sailing: Force 3, perhaps 4, and at last the sunshine was due to return.

'Rich, you got sun cream on? That nose of yours, it won't take anymore punishment this week – if it gets any redder they'll be using you as a marker buoy!'

'Yeah, yeah, yeah; stop mothering me.' And with that they headed out to the race course.

The penultimate race of the championship was completed with little in the way of controversy or incident, except that the winner's podium continued to elude the boys. Worryingly, they continue to drop places in the final sector. It was the same pattern in the fourth race. From first to third place, then they lost another clutch on the last leg. The mood was low.

'What a complete bollocks. What a disaster,' said Richard, and Jonny had to agree.

Sailing back to the beach, Richard was silent. His head was compressed into his shoulders. He had adopted a slumped, fatalistic position. The only brightness in the boat, according to Jonny, seemed to be the luminosity of his nose.

Richard was pensive: concerned, worried and, it seemed, going backwards. A formula to find another gear remained out of their reach. Nevertheless, he refused to accept the inevitable. He knew he couldn't let it get under his skin. But he was truly starting to feel the pressure. It was something that he had never really experienced before; certainly not to this extent. He kept saying to himself: *Can't let Jonny down, can't let those buddies back home down; I'm better than this,* we're *better that this, we're better than all of them out here.*

But for all his efforts at positive thinking, Richard was tense. He knew he must rid himself of any sense of defeatism. He had to allow his mind and body to breathe again. But how?

Then, as they solemnly sailed past the ____ and into the harbour –
Hallelujah! Standing on the slipway beside their boat trolley was not
only Penny, but Samantha too. Richard could feel his head
overheating; perhaps it was sunburn. Jonny, however, was his usual
suave Mr Cool as he glided over to Penny. With one hand he took
the trolley, with the other he pulled her onto him for a welcoming
embrace – and she didn't even get wet.

'How did he do that, the smooth git?' Richard mused. The boys
received pecks on their respective cheeks. Perhaps there was a God
after all, Richard thought, his sombre mood evaporating. The
foursome made light of tucking the 'mistress' away for the night. A
quick change out of their sailing gear allowed for the consumption
of late afternoon cocktails; then the company split. The boys broke
away for showering and toiletries and Penny made haste for the
VW, but not before Samantha had delivered a full-on liquid kiss,
smack on Richard's unprepared lips. Rendezvous times were
synchronised and parting courtesies exchanged.

They met up back at the marquee. But before the evening got
underway, the skipper insisted on going though his daily routine.
Samantha acted as bodyguard. He was unaware of her protection
measures as he commenced his note-taking. He assured her that it
wouldn't take too long. She seemed fairly content.

Race 4	Helm & crew	Race 1	Race 2	Race 3	Accum. points.	After discarded race
1st	Smith & O'Reilly	7th	7th	7th	$21\frac{3}{4}$	$14\frac{3}{4}$
2^{n}	R & G Wilson	42nd	23rd	16th	N/A	N/A
3rd	Owen & Graham	12th	20th	11th	46	26
4th	Marsden & Staunton	6th	5th	5th	20	14
5th	Nixon & Dempsey	27th	10th	57th	99	42
6th	Simms & Prendergast	10th	3rd	6th	25	15
7th	Brett & Martin	27th	10th	13th	57	30
8th	O'Brien Brothers	1st	4nd	10th	22 3/4	$12\frac{3}{4}$
9th	**D'Arcy & Dubois**	4th	8th	2nd	23	14
10th	Hartley-Smyth & Lewis	8th	50th	9th	77	27

Results from Race 4

As a direct consequence of the unsettled conditions afloat, the overall championship position, he noted was somewhat confused. However in relatively short time he had compressed it all down to the final half dozen or so challengers. She was impressed with his mental arithmetic.

Other than for Andy Smith, it was not a great day for any of the budding champions in that penultimate race. More importantly though, Richard's sums had added up to one reality: there was still everything to play for. That fact returned him to a positive, well, relatively positive frame of mind.

'It seems,' he said to Samantha, 'that regardless of how hard we try to eliminate ourselves from this title race, we remain in the running. Hallelujah!'

He continued: 'What a crazy day it was out there. One moment the wind was up, then it would drop and shift direction. Not what the forecasters promised at all. I mean, look at those placings Sam, it's completely spun the championship on its head. Oh boy, it's going to be a big straight and open race to the finish.'

The results board was testament. He turned back to the board, gazed with some sadness at the absence among the leaders of the defending champions, Dave and Michael. They got T-boned just after the start and were forced to retire; their defence in tatters, Dave's beautiful boat sullied. He wondered briefly whether Dave would dive into the drink, or pack up and head home. Richard, for all the right reasons, hoped that he would choose the latter. His mind drifted back to the conversation that he and Michael had on Tuesday evening. Would he tell him or would he leave it until all the fuss had died down? Watch this space, he told himself.

'Hello? Anyone at home?' Richard was in his private world again.

'Sorry Sam, still running sums through my little brain. What were you saying?'

'Nothing nothing of any importance Dearest ...'

A trace of impatience registered in Samantha's voice. Richard, for once, caught her drift, and he presented her with his reasoning. She studied him. He wasn't himself tonight. He was distant, frosty even.

'And that is why I must analyse these results,' he said finally, continuing with his calculations. 'I have to be sure that I know where the danger will come from tomorrow. Mind, the way I feel at the moment I think my biggest problem is inside my own head. I just cannot get around it!'

Samantha was visibly taken aback by his negativity. Up until now she had only ever seen the boyish and brash side of Richard. She studied him again. They found a quiet table. He transferred his notes and calculations into a table format. He proceeded to point out to her the varying permutations. She was stroking his neck. She could feel his tenseness. She remained quiet, awaiting the final, final, result. She was impressed by the maturity of it. She admired the serious, determined personality that was revealing itself. Yes, and of course she also knew – she always had known – that she had made a correct decision this week...

Overall, after Race 4	Total nett points (after discard)	Helm & crew
Leader	12¾	O'Brien brothers
=2nd	14	**D'Arcy & Dubois**
=2nd	14	Burton & Duffy
=2nd	14	Marsden & Staunton
5th	14¾	Smith & O'Reilly
=6th	15	Isherwood twins
=6th	15	Simms & Prendergast

Overall after Race 4 with the worst results discarded.

Richard extracted himself and his head from the notes, the exercise at last complete.

'I'll double check my sums in the morning, but here it is.'

It was a work of art, a table accompanied by suitable graffiti – comments on his final competitors. It was in code but clearly cited each one's weakness, and strengths. He looked deep into Samantha's eyes and in a somewhat subdued tone, confided:

'This is a really tight fight pet, and after today's bollocks, I'm starting to doubt my ability to pull it off – so many people are depending on us.' Samantha turned to him, raised her right hand to his cheek. She gently swivelled him towards her. Tenderly she pressed her lips onto his cheek, whispering into his ear.

'Enough! You, my little Richard, you *can* do this; so come on, I've got a surprise a-waiting.' Grabbing his hand she whisked him away. He stuffed his masterpiece into the hip pocket of his pinstriped blue hipsters. All of them – Penny, Jonny and Richard – piled into her new yellow Beetle and headed off for the grand metropolis of Torquay.

Unbeknownst to either Jonny or Richard, the girls had organised a meal at an uptown restaurant– perhaps it was to be their last supper. The four friends flowed easily from the car, to the restaurant and back to the club, and the conversation and banter flowed with them.

7: Could It Get Any Better?

They returned to the marquee just after the nightly prize giving had concluded. Yet another band had struck up. This time it was a local five piece outfit, The Esler-Burke Blues Band. They were in full fettle. So hit the dance floor they all did, with gusto.

Samantha was off Daddy-sitting duties tonight. These had been delegated within the family. So the loved-up couple had all night to finally get to know each other. Could it get any better? Richard, finally de-stressed, was already on cloud nine and Jonny had joined him there. Samantha and Richard danced, they chatted, she introduced him to her friends and fellow club members. He hardly had time to draw breath. But the place was getting really packed. It had become one massive sardine sandwich. He whispered:

'Umm...fancy getting some air?'

'Thought you'd never ask.' And with that they quietly slipped away. Hand-in-hand they strolled past the clubhouse frontage. They picked their way along the south pier of the little harbour. The night was still. A half moon was playing hide-n-seek with the slow-moving clouds. Long shadows painted watery reflections among the harbour moorings. Richard was grateful for the backdrop of driving blues music bursting from the marquee. It drowned out the sound of his pounding heart.

Samantha, after two unsettling years tinged with personal grief and frustration, had finally reeled her prize boy closer. She was excited and expectant, wondering what the next chapter of *her* championship fairytale would bring. She too was grateful for the decibel levels beating their rhythm across the flat, silvery bay.

There was an overriding air of apprehension and nervousness. It enveloped them. Who was going to make the first move? Both were tense, coiled, ready to embrace – nay, crush – the other.

Richard finally released his hand from her grip. He slipped his arm around her waist. She turned, smiled and reciprocated. She hooked her thumb into his belt, her fingers reaching into his hipster pocket, touching his…race notes.

Almost at the end of the pier, they paused. For all the beauty around them neither, at that moment, had nature's tapestry in mind. Their eyes met. They locked. They were drowning in a passionate embrace. He could feel her heart pumping against his chest. Her lips were moist; she tasted of strawberry – lipstick, or the after-taste of desert? Their first full kiss was electrifying – until their teeth collided. She pulled away, laughed. Then she pressed him gently against the harbour wall. Placing her cold hands on his cheeks she drew herself closer. With one sensuous movement, lips were again dovetailed. Their kissing had become more intense and passionate. They hardly gave themselves time to draw breath.

The moon, on cue, excused itself behind a building cloudbank. Curious male hands, tentatively at first, began to explore. Samantha repositioned herself against the harbour wall, her back resting squarely against a life belt box. Lightly his fingers sculpted her exquisite outlines. Samantha was a willing recipient. She caressed his neck. Breathing quickened. She sighed, exhaling her warm breath onto his neck. She pulled herself ever closer; gently kissed his ear.

Oh my God, this is it – there's no going back now, Richard thought. Then he checked himself. It occurred to him that for the first time in his string of romantic interludes, he wasn't sure he wanted this to become another one-night stand.

Samantha, too, was well aware of his rising passion, and with sudden clarity she questioned what the ultimate outcome of this reckless journey might be. She ached for him. She had ached long and hard. But her mind was a blur. *Was she the… the compass, leading them down this path of no return?* She told herself firmly: *I am not a one-night-stand. I am not easy!* She demanded of herself some self-control, enough to slow her runaway emotions.

Richard too was in turmoil; after all this time of waiting would this, *could* this dissolve into another fleeting holiday romance?

Would it fizzle out all together, along with his title challenge? He little realised that his emotions were in concert with Samantha's. He, however, was being driven by an altogether greater force...

You can't stop now; you must go with it. She wants you... Richard's opportunist hormones were now in the driver's seat. They overrode all semblance of emotional control. He was flying blind, his decision processes on testosterone-fuelled autopilot. He had, in fact, little meaningful thought process, and less control. *Oh God,* he thought*, is this really happening? This doesn't feel right.* He wrestled with his demons, and somehow, from somewhere, he gathered a veneer of self-control.

This is too fast. Stop, stop – must stop.

Samantha, too, with a rising sense of panic, was beginning to come to her senses. But she dithered. *I want him; I really want him. But I want him forever. I want* – the realisation came as something of a shock – *to grow old with him.* She tried to take a mental step back. *I've got to stop this. But oh my God, will he? What will I do if he continues? What, for that matter, will I do if he walks away?* On the brink of allowing nature to take its course, she delayed. By now her top was fully undone, and as his intentions were telegraphed southwards, she gave a little gasp. Then purposefully, gently, she took his wrist and whispered:

'Hove to, sailor. Not tonight – it's lady time.' It took Richard only a moment to understand what she was saying. A clock stopper. A moment when, for the first time in his randy life, he was actually relieved, compliant, almost embarrassed. She smiled. He politely looked away as she delicately did up that which he had undone. Together, they breathed a timely sigh of relief. Without words, they agreed that what had just occurred was far too much, far too soon.

She was more than relieved; she was joyous. Okay, she had uttered a little white lie – she had taken a chance. Was it calculated? It didn't matter because now, she knew. For Samantha, 'I love you' was no longer a casual term of endearment. She really had fallen hook line and sinker for this boy. She was in love, full, complete and absolute! And what's more, she knew he felt the same about her – she just knew.

With a purposeful clench she then pulled him back to her. Passion was re-ignited, but with soft and subtle tenderness. Then they were quiet again. Richard was weak, drifting; he had never been submerged in such emotion. It was alien to him. *I'm in love. Am I in love? I must be…*

Fergal O'Brien and Miss Hartley-Smyth passed by into the night. Richard, recovering some sense of the moment, said:

'Now that's what's called an Anglo Irish agreement.'

But Samantha was miles away. She turned, looked at him quizzically. He offered an explanation, but she was somewhere else. He tried a new tack.

'It's 1975. He's over here, in England…' He expected her to have shared his appetite for daily news. She just smiled. She wondered dreamily if her actions had left him a little dizzy.

'Come on sailor, you owe me the last dance.' She kissed him again, and they headed to the marquee for the last set. The band had struck up with a classic: 'Satisfaction'.

'Sam, I don't believe this is happening,' he mouthed to her above the decibels. 'They're playing my anthem. Another omen maybe?' A perfect ending to a perfect evening, he thought to himself.

They strolled back to Samantha's Beetle, parked some way along the esplanade. Under the intermittent cascade from a faulty street lamp, he kissed her a passionate goodnight. She wished him luck for the final race. They kissed again, and she drove off into the Devon night. He floated back to the campsite. He sung his personal version of the anthem, '*I've really got my sat-is-faction...*' He forgot they had visitors, grunted an apology, the simultaneous flash of female flesh didn't register; he crawled into the little tent and fell into a most luxurious sleep. Only to be awaked by:

'Hey lover boy, any chance you could drag yourself away from Samantha and join us for breakfast?' It was Jonny's morning wakeup call.

'Very funny.' But he couldn't help checking if indeed she was beside him – disappointed, he made himself respectable and joined them.

'Penny, you're a pleasure to wake up to under this perfect Wedgewood sky.'

'Ricky, you're full of shit.'

'He's put you up to that – the name's Richard.' They laughed, and Richard knew nothing could annoy him today – he was at peace with the world. Jonny was fairly chirpy too – had he enjoyed an equally romantic night with the lovely Penny. Richard's visual blot of the previous night's encounter suddenly flashed; he smiled but said nothing.

8: Championship:
Final Day (Friday)

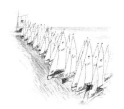

With Johnny's goodbye rituals completed, they strode off purposefully in the direction of the club grounds. They presented themselves like Vikings, poised for further conquests. On arrival at the dinghy park they carried out a meticulous survey of the good ship *Satisfaction.* They inspected for anything which could ultimately fail or snag; the last thing needed was for their dependable mistress to unravel on this, the last day of the championship.

Failure to complete this, the most important race of the series, would represent a disaster of Titanic proportions – memories of last year's debacle continue to haunt them. Happy that their craft was indeed seaworthy, their next stop was the published weather forecast. This, as usual, was posted on the official notice board alongside the huge results display. Richard risked a glance at their overnight standing.

Jonny was a little more juvenile, nudging and pointing out the obvious to his skipper...

But Richard wasn't biting. 'At last,' he said, 'some wind.'

Jonny failed to give this statement his full attention. Behind the boyish facade he remained a little perturbed.

'I'll catch you up. Just want to recheck something skipper.' He didn't mention that he had found one of the connectors – which effectively held up the rig – to be partially undone. He was suspicious that they had been sabotaged; he was certain that he'd checked this yesterday after the race. Maybe he was wrong; however, he proceeded to recheck *all* essential parts before rejoining his skipper. No mention was made of his suspicions, as Richard clearly had enough on his plate. The forecast was indicating Force 3–4, and warning of a possible Force 5–6 later. Richard persuaded Jonny to focus on the weather front shown on the chart and Jonny, in turn, digested it. He was now in race mode.

'This'll sort the men from the boys,' he said. 'Mate, be prepared, it could get really wild and windy out there.'

Jonny nodded, attempted a smile. He was keen to get afloat, but Richard remained hesitant, whether through nerves or apprehension about the weather, Jonny couldn't figure. He just hoped that the goings-on of last night had not scrambled his skipper's competitive head – for the moment, his race head seemed to be attached, but Jonny wasn't at all sure whether it was screwed tightly onto his torso…

Richard then excused himself. He headed off for a final, nerve-induced call of nature, and to recheck his calculations. He needed some privacy, a little space. He must ensure that in the event of a close finish he was absolutely clear which crews could ultimately beat them. He was continually reminded, haunted, by the regatta, where in similar circumstances they picked the wrong target.

Thank God I can add up whilst watching the wind change, he told himself.

This final day had dawned well enough for them. They had been focused, but relaxed. Probably in the most relaxed mood of the week. They had agreed that their best strategy was to sail a conservative race; to distance *Satisfaction* from unnecessary confrontation. They especially needed to avoid the attentions of those competitors who were closest to them on the overall points standing; all six of them! That count included club mates Burton & Duffy. A pre-race home club gathering was convened just outside the clubhouse. Twelve arms rested on shoulders and a group huddle was formed. Hands were shaken and best wishes offered. It was a fairly emotional affair but the competitive tension and pre-race nerves made it a brief encounter.

As things stood they were equal second overall, but alongside two other crews. Even if they were to retire from this race, the worst Richard D'Arcy & Jonny Dubois would finish overall would be seventh. In itself that would not be a bad result. This was their homecoming fallback plan – their Plan B, unconvincing as it was, should it all go awry.

Even though their previous outings had not been without difficulties, they knew they had the ability to pull it off. It wouldn't be easy, but they realised that each of the other competing crews were going through the same issues. It was theirs to win, not lose. No countenance of 'B' plan would be tolerated.

Richard D'Arcy was finally ready for battle. The sail-out to the starting area took a little over half an hour, and whilst they were cautious, they also revelled in the lively breeze. It presented a perfect opportunity to get loosened up, to regain their sea legs. Everything was going to plan until Richard's concentration momentarily wavered. He allowed the boat to screw up off the back of a wave in an unexpected gust of wind. Result: they laid *Satisfaction* flat on the water.

They were awash, capsized alongside the varnished hull of the 45 foot long race control vessel anchored in the day's designated starting area. Its crew cheered. Jonny was not receptive; he was over the side in a flash, his feet on the exposed centre board, levering the boat upright. Richard, meanwhile, had lost his grip and slipped off the side deck into the flooded cockpit.

'Bloody water's freezing'.

'Serves you right, suppose you were with Samantha again...'

He couldn't muster an immediate reply. The temperature of the water had literally taken his breath away but he also knew that Jonny was right. With the boat again upright and baled, he turned to Richard.

'So, we'll not be performing that manoeuvre again.'

The skipper didn't answer.

The breeze settled down again. It was blowing steady and with purpose – Richard reckoned it was at the top end of Force 3. It was time to check out the first leg of the course, and because of their earlier indiscretion they had only limited time for this very necessary exercise.

Within the starting zone the countdown had commenced. The day was in perfect shape. It promised champagne sailing. The brisk breeze had created a choppy but manageable sea-state. The bay sparkled in the noon sunshine.

The sound of the cannon had got the final proceedings of the week under way; then another cloud of smoke and a low crack opened an all too familiar scenario.

'Oops – someone is out of the blocks too early, and it's certainly not us. Not one of your classic starts, skipper.'

A 'second row' starting position had not dealt them a great opening hand for their final battle! But Richard and Jonny quickly realised that their mediocre beginning to this the final, and crucial, race of the series had been a gift for the favourites Simms & Prendergast, and indeed the other contenders too.

Even worse, Jonny noticed that club mates Alan Burton and Paddy Duffy were also off to a good start.

'Sorry mate, I was too cautious,' was Richard's belated and somewhat despondent answer.

'Look, were not out of it,' he said, 'but we're in a bit of trouble here. We've gotta get out of this lane and into a clear wind-stream. So at the first opportunity we tack, OK?'

'Understood.' Jonny remained pumped up. Richard glanced around, saw a gap. He immediately called:

'Ready about!' Aggressively, he swung *Satisfaction* through the wind onto port tack. They drove her hard to source that clear air. Jonny, in his crewing role, was efficiently (so he thought) relaying information about the traffic and goings-on around them.

Unfortunately, his words were lost on Richard, who was elsewhere; an ear-to-ear grin and a general feeling of warmth and well-being were ample testament. Even after downing gulps of sea water in the earlier capsize, he could yet inhale the fragrance of her perfume –'Charlie', he believed.

S-T-A-R-B-O-A-R-D!!

In a blinding flash Richard decoded what Jonny reported a moment earlier. He had warned of an incoming craft on the starboard – the 'right of way' – tack. Richard had a matter of seconds to decide on an appropriate anti-collision measure. Only two options were available., and either would be a major manoeuvre. He could bear off sharply and risk clipping the incoming boat's aft quarter, or they could crash-tack *Satisfaction* back onto their previous tack. The former was far too risky. It needed more space and space was not in abundance. They crash-tacked...

This, however, left them wallowing, starved of propulsion. It created an unnecessary hurdle in an already tough scenario. To get back to at least even terms with the favourites would take nothing short of superhuman effort, never mind luck.

'We're screwed.'

Richard was utterly deflated. His posture matched his tone. Although the sun had lit up Torbay, for them it was the dark side of the moon. The ultimate silverware had been within touching distance. In a lapse of concentration it had been wrested away for at least another year. And worse, their club mates had remained in the hunt...

What a complete bollocks...

He was submerged in self-pity. Ahead lay a steep, nay, vertical uphill task, a torturous two and a half hours of racing.

What's the point? Why finish the championship challenge wallowing in the wake of those leaders; yesterday's competitors? Go home boys, you're a beaten docket.

Unable to help himself, Jonny started on him. Richard had never seen him so angry; he'd never even heard him swear before.

'Rich-ARD, you complete dick. For fucks sake, will you waken up? What the hell's going on? Where's your bleedin' head this day?' He slammed his fists onto the deck. 'We were trying to win this fuckin race! "Nothing else will do" – remember?'

Jonny's uncharacteristic rant shocked master D'Arcy back into reality. It was harsh but fair.

They sailed on, and as they rounded the first mark of the course their dilemma once more hit home – 23rd place or worse. The boat had been very quiet for the entirety of that opening leg. There were no angels hovering above them this time. No heavenly assistance to lift them out of the doldrums. Richard privately measured the reality of the situation: seamanship and superhuman effort alone would not suffice. His attention turned heavenwards, in search of a Torbay miracle...

Yes Richard, you've really screwed up big time this time. Not Jonny, you – on your very own. What a complete dick. All the hard work flushed down the toilet. You are the bollocks of the day – of the century!

In a last ditch attempt to lighten the mood, Richard turned to Jonny:

'Look mate, I know I've let you down and fucked up our adventure, so if you want we can sail home now and get offside. Or, we can have some fun down this off-wind leg.' His tone was apologetic, but not entirely defeatist. 'That weather system I showed you earlier is almost upon us– there is a big wind a-coming.'

Richard was down, but deep within him stirred the natural competitor, urging him, albeit in a whisper, not to give up. He hoped, he prayed that his shipmate had similar stirrings. Of course he was all too aware that if they were to stand any chance of respectable showing he would have to get things back into perspective – competitive instinct first, love-sick idiot second.

The cloud was starting to lift….

'Aah, we're both to blame,' said Jonny, ever the diplomat. 'Okay, why not? Let's go for it; boys together, no babes - OK? The nearly team need to inject some fun back into their day.'

With that they rounded the windward mark and set their course. But this time Richard steered higher than the fleet – it looked more like an armada – ahead of them. They hoisted their quartered orange and purple spinnaker, trimmed it and waited...

Richard D'Arcy wore a devilish, perhaps devil-may-care, smirk. He knew they had nothing to lose.

9: In the Zone

But the sport of competitive sailing is a funny old game. Tides and shifting winds can turn a race course inside-out in the blink of a bursting cloud. As the fleet had populated the starting area earlier that day, even the least observant among the 160 or so crews could not fail to have noticed that there was a change in the air...

That sparkling starting area, which had enjoyed a perfect 12-knot southwest by west breeze, would soon be engulfed by a towering menacing curdling grey cloudbank. It had already exposed a little of its rumbling signature to the zigzagging fleet as it tacked up the first leg of the course towards the windward marker. The more experienced crews were preparing themselves; an altogether bigger wind was on the way.

The Devon sun, which earlier had bathed the course with its warming rays, had dimmed. The temperature had dropped too. The change would be swift, certainly swifter than the forecasters had predicted. Was it possible, wondered Richard, that the changing conditions might produce a lifeline? The odds would suggest otherwise, but when the odds were stacked against them, any thread menacing or otherwise, was worth grasping.

Then it hit them; a gust like a shockwave from a bomb blast. Spindrift contrasted with the dark and fractious sea. There was a roar in the air and the sounds of thrashing sail cloth all around them.

The boat lurched dramatically to leeward. Instinctively Richard and Jonny countered by shifting their wetsuit-clad bodies up onto the windward side deck. Their ankles bit into the two-inch wide foot-strap webbing. And with bodies straining, *Satisfaction* was levered back to the vertical. Like a bolt from a bow, she catapulted off downwind. By steering across and down the building waves, surfboard-fashion, Richard worked the tiller in harmony with Jonny's sail-trimming and sheer athleticism. Their craft accelerated, gaining noticeably on that leading fleet.

Bouncing, it seemed, from wave to wave with audible booms and whooshes, *Satisfaction* was forced over and through any watery obstacles the conditions presented. At times they were sailing on instinct and feel. Walls of solid spray frequently engulfed them.

They were undoubtedly in the zone. As the next turning marker came into sight through the silver spray, Richard reckoned they had made up ten places – in just one leg.

Although they could now see the leading bunch, this was the infamous gybe-marker – a zone often referred to in racing as the sailor's graveyard. The point in the race whereupon each craft performs a dramatic change in direction, where the blowing breeze gets transferred from one side of the boat to the other; the sails crash across with venomous energy. Straight forward enough in a light breeze, but when the conditions are ratcheted up, as indeed they were in this the final race of the championship even the leaders – especially the leaders, with much to forfeit – could not be laxed. The wind had already increased to close to forecast, and seemed unlikely to slacken. There had been several capsizes. Crews caught out by the viciousness of the gusts clung to their upturned craft, their final day prematurely over.

But with the zone imminent they determined, in their new-found confidence that they were not going to join the casualty list. In concert and in clockwork, they prepared to roll out their much-practiced routine for this most precarious of manoeuvres:

Bear off – pick the wave – accelerate – balance and turn the boat – slam the sails through the wind – re-trim – sit out hard over her new windward side – drive the boat aggressively to get clear of any close-by competitors.

Dead easy. They did it – three others didn't. Richard and Jonny eyeballed each other, just for an instant: it was a moment of triumph, of satisfaction, and of relief. A micro moment. They careered down the second off-wind leg of the course, again at high speed. They were now in 10th place. As the wind continued to build they found that they were not only opening the gap on the boats astern but closing fast on a bunch of five or six boats roughly 45 yards – some nine boat-lengths – in front of them.

'Come on Rich,' Johnny yelled, 'we can get into these guys. Harder, faster! Faster, sit out further!'

Richard's legs were aching. His eyes were burning with salt. Adrenalin was king as he strained to match his partner's agility and fitness level. They were a crew on fire. In what was edging towards extreme surfing conditions their spinnaker was straining at every seam. Few of the teams ahead had chanced flying a spinnaker. They stormed ever closer. The bunch was now well within their sights – only six boat-lengths away. Little *Satisfaction* was travelling so fast now that her grey hull must, it felt to Richard at the helm, be clean out of the water at times.

The whole boat was vibrating, humming; it felt as though they'd never sailed so aggressively or gone so fast over the water.

But Richard's immediate thought was, *How in the name of Neptune are we going to slow her down for the next turning marker?* An air of foreboding consumed him. He tried to refocus.

'Yes, mate, I'm really crapping myself,' he said aloud as Johnny wrestled the spinnaker, squeezing from it every last ounce of drive. Suddenly there was drama ahead. Through the blinding spray, which was making vision almost impossible, they saw a blue sail hit the water in spectacular fashion. As they raced past, a stolen glance revealed a broken mast, snapped like a twig in these boiling conditions. Jonny said;

'One less to concern us.'

'Don't tempt bleedin providence mate.'

Rather that push their luck, they doused their coloured sail early, and prepared to round the fast approaching mark. No time for heroics.

They had also achieved one of their objectives; they were knocking at the back door of the bunch. If they could execute a good rounding, another brace of places was theirs for the taking.

Richard rolled out his plan. He could see that within this tight bunch, and considering the conditions, there was going to be more than a little carnage as they all narrowed in on the turning point.

'Jonny, it is vital that we escape from this rounding, clean and clear.'

Richard's instruction was perfectly understood.

'Okay skip – one step at a time, no manic moves.'

There were still six legs of this final race to complete. But by the way they felt, especially since the earlier frost had dissolved, anything was doable.

'Must continue to play safe, to remain upright,' said Richard. 'I've done my swimming for today.'

Jonny forced a grin. Yes, that D'Arcy/Dubois confidence had returned. More especially, Richard's concentration was again 110 percent, at least while they remained at sea...

It needed to be. In those conditions one lapse would surely have pulled down the curtain on their adventure. *Samantha, sorry girl, I've work to do out her*e.

Their mark rounding was impeccable. And indeed there was carnage. One capsized – the O'Brien's hardened in too aggressively and got blown over. Then a dramatic collision between the sailboats of Marsden and Burton. The Burton boat suffered a stoved in side and was forced to retire, their championship chase over. Another sailor had missed their straps. They believed it was Alison Firth – she went clean over the side. It was certainly all happening. But for once the boys were quite happy not to have been invited to that particular party.

From their revised viewing station the wind again bit into their faces – they had rounded up into the next windward leg. Ahead, Jonny relayed a spectacular seascape of white-capped waves but no longer an armada of white sails. They were a further three places to the good.

From mediocre, even negative beginnings, the day had just got better and better. Another gruelling upwind leg was completed but without further gains. They were upright and they were positive again, a positivity which had the effect of numbing their brains to pain. In normal circumstances their superhuman workload should have had manifested itself in muscle fatigue, even cramp. But, fighting not only the cold and stinging saltwater but the wind which threatened with every gust to flatten their craft, Richard and Jonny's dream had been revived. Driven, Richard continued to steer expertly up over and around the angry seaway. It had boiled up waves so high that at times the boats ahead were lost in its troughs. Jonny was in concert, his six feet of athletic frame continuing to lever and maintain the boat at an upright angle. This greatly assisted the helmsman in mastering the elements.

Jonny was reminded of a piece of theory that Richard had handed down on the maiden voyage, those many seasons ago: *Small plywood sailing dinghies, unlike classic yachts portrayed in works of art, do not sail efficiently when heeled over.* This was the fuel that fed his efforts and maintained *Satisfaction* as an upright, fast and efficient craft.

They continued to close down the competition. But how long could they keep up their charge; just how full were their physical batteries?

Ahead, Jonny could now clearly see that the race was led by the white boat of John Simms and Julian Prendergast. They were only marginally ahead of the Isherwood twins in their matching red attire. Andy Smith and Fran O'Reilly, a bit further back, were in third place. It was with some misgivings, therefore, that Jonny relayed this information to his skipper. This was exactly what they didn't want to see – as things stood all these crews were now on superior scores. Harsh though it was, they had to face up to the fact that their charge to the front had, in effect, hit the buffers. Richard spoke across the boat to Jonny.

'Any bright ideas mate? Can you see a way through this lot?'

There was a pause before a pensive Jonny replied, somewhat offhandedly:

'You're the skipper, and the brains... I'm just the muscle.'

In normal circumstances a negative quip like that could have short-circuited, even extinguished, a sportsman's competitive drive. But Jonny was no fool. He knew exactly which of Richard's buttons to press. There was, he hoped, a reserve tank yet to be tapped. Of course he had now played his final card. Whether it was an ace or a joker remained to be seen. But he had an unbending confidence, believing that his skipper could wriggle them out of this aquatic conundrum.

Jonny was, indeed, the muscle; but on that day, with the wind steadily easing, mental as opposed to physical fitness would emerge as the key ingredient – combined, of course, with the aforementioned athletic brilliance, outstanding stamina, aquatic technique and, Jonny was forced to admit, blind confidence.

When they finally rounded that leeward mark, and after a downwind sail devoid of any real drama other than some dramatic looking rolls and lurches among the huge breaking waves, they were elated to find that *Satisfaction* was now among that hitherto leading pack. D'Arcy and Dubois had moved up to fifth place! They had also closed the gap on the Simms &Prendergast boat.

As they entered the final windward leg of the course, the wind shifted noticeably. It began to oscillate; some five degrees to port, then to starboard, at intervals of five to ten minutes. Jonny glanced at his skipper. He reckoned he could actually hear cogs turning. He smiled inwardly, awaited his instructions. He knew that it was all about to kick off. His head spun with anticipation: thoughts, of glory, of failure. It was the glory though which swamped his natural ability to focus. In a flash, somehow his boyhood days in the Staffordshire Boys Brigade rushed to the fore; of the church outings, the hymn – their anthem – and the words of one particular verse: *Will your eyes behold through the morning light the city of gold and the harbour light... We have an anchor...*But just as quickly as the brainstorm appeared, Jonny had returned to action stations.

Wind shifts mean lots off assertive tacks, which in turn equate to nautical short-cuts. The leading bunch, all of them close-hauled on the wind, had committed to sailing out onto the starboard side of this final leg. It had previously been seen as the favoured side of the course. It had brought about race wins for the O'Brien's, John Simms and Dave Gilmore. But this change in wind direction was telling Richard D'Arcy a different tale, and considering their position, he had little option but to listen.

So he tacked *Satisfaction* around again and sailed off to the opposite course-side to find fortune, or their final demise. Their old lake-sailing techniques had come into play – techniques they had developed to maximise every whisper of wind which filtered onto the water through the Long Lake's tree-lined shores. They instinctively tacked to and fro in concert with the instability of the shifting wind. They sensed that they were making ground. Their focus, however, had to be on the leading trio of boats.

Both Richard and Jonny were wise enough to realise that given the distance, probably a couple of hundred yards apart, an early gain could so easily revert to the status quo. Eventually the breeze did settle. It also dropped back to a soft Force 4: ten knots, no more than twelve, they reckoned.

And so, it came to the acid test. They prepared to tack across to confront the pack.

Converging at an angle of some 45 degrees, even the most visually impaired seadog could not deny that their position had much improved: neither Richard nor Jonny could believe by just how much! The building audience of spectator craft sensed that something special was about to happen: binoculars were trained, cameras focused. An air of anticipation, of silent excitement, had descended over the bay. They couldn't, could they…?

'Crikey, skipper, we've cleaned them!' Jonny's earlier experiments in reverse psychology had elicited the performance, the never-say-die attitude, he had hoped for. Luck had nothing to do with it, he assured himself.

'Not all of them mate, but enough to be getting on with.' The skipper knew there was still a job to do. While they would clearly cross ahead of the red boat of Smith and, this new third place would actually do them no favours in the final analysis.

The dark clouds had for the most part passed over the race course but even with the wind eased, it remained unstable. Richard and Jonny glanced at each other, fire burning in their blue eyes, and as one, they mentally agreed: we can do this!

They went into high-speed conference mode. They worked out that of the two boats ahead of them, John Simms, skippering the white boat, was still leading. He and Julian were barely holding off the ever-advancing Isherwood's – they had painted their boat red on one side and a lime green on the other. Welsh colours, but boy was it confusing at times, thought Richard. He also thought, hoped, that these boats would remain locked in a two-horse race.

'They'll be blinded by a personal attack-defend duel,' he said calmly to Jonny. 'Hopefully they'll remain locked like dogs in heat right to the finishing line.' As Jonny gave him one of his looks he continued: 'And you know something, mate? We'll not interrupt them.'

'Yeah, let them sail their own race and we'll sail ours.' Jonny concurred.

Mindful that Andy & Fran, although behind them, were still a danger, for Richard it was all or nothing now. Having sailed on for some ten minutes, he declared:

'Fuck it Jonny, we really have nothing to lose and everything to gain. Let's just go for it, let's go NOW.'

He had hardly finished his 'state of the nation' declaration when the wind suddenly shifted; their compass indicated that it had headed almost ten degrees. Instinctively they tacked around and realised immediately that the leading boats were … leading no more.

As their new course tracked across, Richard's mind went into mathematical overdrive. He had to be sure that his own personal sums were indeed correct. Yep, the way things stood a win would give them 14¾ points against Simms and Prendergast with 17 points, and the Isherwood's would end the week with 18 points. He released a newsflash.

'Jonny, here's the position. If we win this race, we win. Being second... means we lose, okay?'

'Message received and understood skipper...' At that, they crossed the bow of the white boat. A rumble of spectator reaction reached across the race course.

All that had to be done now was to protect and defend their new position by executing a covering tack and setting their winning boat on a victory course towards the finishing line. Billy and Fran, who had opted to follow in *Satisfaction's* wake, also made up so much ground they challenged the Isherwood's third place, the apparent dead-heat being resolved in favour of the former and adding to a spectacle which would be remembered as the most exciting championship finale the fleet, and indeed the race officials, had ever witnessed.

Manoeuvre complete – it was probably the sweetest and smoothest roll-tack they'd ever performed. Not a flap from the jib. Jonny, in ballet mode, hooked his ankles under the straps and together they hiked their torsos over her side to lever their dancing boat upright. Their sails reset, they accelerated towards their first ever national title. Only a handful of yards to the finishing buoy now...

But the next thing Richard D'Arcy remembered was a floating sensation in a salty green haze. He was coughing up what appeared to be half the English Channel!

10: The Final Push!

Richard's world had somersaulted seawards in slow motion. He knew instinctively that he'd missed his straps. He back-flipped like a trapeze artist – the only difference being the absence of a safety net. His last glimpse was of the white boat; Jonny later swore that he heard them sniggering – even above the anguished roar from the spectators, and his skipper.

'No, no, NO! I've handed it all back to them, on a plate.' Richard was still calculating points when he hit the water. Most of his tirade of f-words was thankfully delivered underwater. He surfaced quickly. Somehow he had managed to hold onto a rope. Furiously, and with bad-tempered determination, he reeled himself back. Above, he could see the outline of Jonny, waving him closer. Their mistress had mercifully remained upright, but was stalled. She remained tantalisingly close, within touching distance of the finishing line.

Richard was instantly on his travels again, this time in an upwards direction. With his trailing arm, Jonny yanked him clean out of the water and with a dull thud, deposited his skipper back into the cockpit. It was a herculean effort. Richard was left 'eating' the bilges, his ankles still dangling over the side. Through a haze, he marvelled. He had no idea how his partner had achieved this feat. Immediately, his automatic gyro engaged, he reverted to the upright. With his left hand back on the tiller, ankles scrambling for grip, and torso re-hiked, *Satisfaction* was back under control. But Richard wasn't. He made a fine attempt at an encore. Jonny was immediately back at the cliff-face. In an instant, they realised that the somersault was not a miss, but the return their gear failure nemesis.

Jonny frowned, puzzled. But he made no comment; there was a race to finish. He merely provided some support, moral and physical, for his skipper.

'Come on Ricky, settle; we need to reach the finishing line.' Up to speed, *Satisfaction* was re-energised, and she accelerated like a stallion out of its stall.

'Drive, drive...' They urged each other on. They had used up their last gasps of energy stolen from residual drips of adrenalin. Of course, they realised that fellow competitors (Richard's description was less prosaic) Simms and Prendergast had slipped out of their grasp. They had crossed the finish line barely half a boat length in front of them. The final cannon of the week had fired, but they felt like mere witnesses, not participants. An aura of silence had again descended over their good ship. Although the closeness of the finish may have been spectacular, for the boys it was hollow. So near but, for practical purposes, so far.... Energy was finally sapped, evaporated.

They silently reflected that in time they would remember this day as the conclusion of a tale of adventure, of drama, and of romance. But in the cold reality of the present it had all been a failure, devoid of romance. Before Richard could express his sincere apologies, Jonny turned to him, his voice low and strained.

'No, no need to skipper – I know.' Then he smiled. 'Look at the state of you – you look as if you've gone ten rounds with Henry Cooper.'

Richard wiped at the blood on his face, realising that it was everywhere; a mess of moving and dark congealed slime . He wiped his hand on his blue and white buoyancy vest and offered it, palm outstretched, to Jonny. They shook – no hugs.

'Right Jonny boy; a big breath, dig deep and bite hard. We've now got to sail over there and congratulate those fuckers.' The skipper was fighting to keep a lid on the sense of disappointment and anguish that they both felt, and to take control of the situation.

'Yeah okay, let's do it.' Jonny was equally crestfallen but he was prepared.

Duty done, they waited for a reaction, but John Simms and Julian Prendergast just looked at them in disbelief, John looking Richard straight in the face, Julian the same with Jonny.

'You must have taken in more than water down there Rickey my man – don't you realise that there was only the one cannon fired? For you guys. We were that recalled boat right at the start of the race. Yep, they finally got me; look, there's my damned sail number displayed loud and clear on the finishing boat.' And then, with proper solemnity, he said:

'And so, you're the new champions!' Julian excitedly interrupted his skipper, and bellowed:

'Three cheers – Hip...' He and John were now standing up in the cockpit of their craft, applauding. They warmly and genuinely congratulated the flabbergasted and still disbelieving duo. At that stage Richard wasn't sure whether it was blood streaming down his face, or tears. To say he was gobsmacked would be an understatement.

He sensed the last of his energy drain from his body. Dropping onto one knee he grabbed the edge of the side deck for balance, visions flooding back of spiralling out over the side, again! Jonny was in a similar state but he just sat there, slumped on the deck. His head was bowed. He kept shaking it from side to side.

Then came the wailing. It was drifting down the wind. Who had appeared but the bold Archie, resplendent in ceremonial kilt? He was standing on the foredeck not of his Dragon but a pretty motor boat of traditional lines, his bagpipes in full bellow. Then the boys realised he was not alone; Penny with Samantha were also on board, waving and cheering, Samantha at the wheel leaning out of the varnished wheelhouse. Coming to his senses, Jonny broke the almost ghostly aura which had engulfed their little craft.

'Ay-e,' he said, mimicking Archie in the background. 'A wee bit like 'Villa scoring in the 89th minute, eh Ricky ?'

Then, face as white as a sheet, he grunted to Richard politely and said very quietly:

'Any chance of getting me ashore? I think ... I've really damaged myself hauling your flying carcass back onboard. Ever thought of losing a few pounds?'

Richard, although grinning, immediately realised that he was not joking. All was not well with his Jonny boy!

'Right, okay, just make yourself as comfortable… it's your shoulder, isn't it?'

'Yeah, I've really pulled something.'

Fearing that Jonny was going to pass out, Richard beckoned to the nearest of the rescue craft. He also called on Archie's crew. He was very much the man in control now. He remembered, of course: Samantha – nurse – emergency – assistance...

Both craft arrived more or less simultaneously, as did John and Julian. Everyone quickly saw that something was wrong. The best option was to transfer Jonny to the rescue boat. It was an open ski-boat. It had been hired from a neighbouring water sports centre for the duration of the championship. It sported a powerful 50hp cream-coloured Evinrude outboard engine. It was fast.

This, Richard determined, would serve as a rapid-to-shore ambulance. The two girls had transferred across, leaving Archie single-handed. Richard had already planned that with Jonny onboard the sports boat, he and Samantha could sail *Satisfaction* home. With an experienced hand, she managed to temporally strap up the troubled shoulder, a length of light rope having been magically produced. As for the Richard's cunning plan, Jonny was having none of it.

'I started the day,' he said, 'in this boat and I'll finish the day, in this boat.'

There was no arguing with him. Samantha glanced at Penny, rolled her eyes and transferred back into the ski- boat. Roger, the driver, took a turn at persuading Jonny, but he wouldn't budge. Penny shouted across:

'You're spending far too much time with that Ricky. You've become big stubborn oaf.'

The tow rope was hitched up between *Satisfaction* and the ski-boat.

As Samantha exited *Satisfaction,* Richard couldn't help but cast an eye across the outline of her exquisite transom. At a compromised pace, the tow made for the beach. Richard steered a-line astern of the support craft. His concentration wavered. His mind was racing in retro. He continued to recount the highs and lows of that crazy, yes crazy, race. He reckoned that such a scenario could have evolved only in a Steve McQueen film. Mid-fleet to the winning post! He just couldn't take it in. Then suddenly he jumped bolt upright. A startled Jonny reacted. A jolt of pain shot through his arm. Richard said:

'Is it a dream?'

*Satisfactio*n went off on a speed wobble – they were travelling even faster, it seemed, than they had in the race – but quickly Richard regained control.

'Oh for goodness sake, sit down you dick.' Jonny, unimpressed, gave out one of his looks.

'Flippin' 'eck mate, I can't believe it. We've actually done it. We did it. Yes, us two against the nation.'

Reality had finally hit Richard smack between the eyes. 'The luck of the Irish, eh?' He was rambling...

'Luck? Luck had nothing to do with it. Jeez Rich when will you ever stop playing the underdog? We were the strongest, fittest, and boldest crew our here today. You were the fastest helmsman; that's why we're the champions. And where's all this Irish nationalism crap coming from? Think you've lost more blood than I thought, Ricky-boy.'

Richard didn't respond. He was thinking; but before he could speak, Jonny was back on him.

'Don't you even think about it. I know exactly what you're thinking; it's that flamin film title.'

'What?'

'You and your black and white movies.'

'What?' Richard was smiling, his mischief making inner sense driving him to wind up his mate more; *Okay, here goes, but I'll just say it once. I will, honest.* Richard drew himself to his feet, the tiller between his knees and arms out-stretched, and at full volume, he let rip;

'Fortune, Jonny — fortune favours the brave.' He got a round of applause and more curious looks from the crew of the rescue craft.

'OK, on this occasion, mate, I'll agree with you, but please, please don't say it again, and especially... at the prize giving tonight. Please.'

Jonny was smiling again. Having returned to the sitting position, Richard reached over and gave his friend a private congratulatory punch on the arm.

'Oh fuck!'

'Oh shit, sorry mate...'

'Oh, get off. Keep your distance, you're a flaming liability today.'

The crew of the rescue boat had overheard, and they glanced around. Jonny, turning his back to the girls leant towards his skipper administering a playful slap on his cheek.

'But you're not too bad at the sailing lark either, Ricky boy.'

Richard nodded and smiled. Jonny's previous grin had now opened into a static smile. There wasn't much colour in his face, unlike Richard's blood-stained mess.

The fast ride to shore was certainly efficient, but it had inflicted a high level of pain and discomfort. Jonny was thinking, but not admitting, that perhaps he had chosen the wrong option. He said, almost to himself:

'Standards. Champions have standards to maintain. This was a team effort and we're that team.'

'What was that, mate?' his skipper enquired.

'Nothing Ricky, you wouldn't understand.'

Jonny was smirking.

The girls were instantaneously out of the rescue boat. *Satisfaction* was quickly hauled onto her trolley. Richard was immediately over the side. He held the boat steady. This allowed Jonny, who was looking a bit better, to swivel his backside and legs out over the side. Feet touched terra firma. Samantha, shoes discarded, was in the water too. She and Penny supported Jonny up the slipway, while the skipper and a gang of club people parked the boat.

Very selfishly, Richard couldn't help thinking he was being ignored, chastised even – and he the one with the gashed face, the tapestry of clotted blood and underneath, no doubt a broken a nose too. All the Jonny boy had was a girly strain and maybe another blister and broken fingernail or two...

But all was soon well again in Richard's world, as a cold wet cloth, with the taste of the sea, was dabbed across his face. Luscious lips followed.

'Look babe,' said Samantha. 'I think the Jonny boy has really hurt himself, so we're going to run him up to Torquay so the docs can have a proper look. I'll catch you later, okay?'

She made to leave, turning to walk backwards as she said: 'I told you, didn't I? I told you, you could do it. Love you — bye.' And she was gone.

Quietly replete, and with a smile that lingered for some time, he got on with the de-rigging of their mistress, their lovely mistress. However, progress was slow. In truth, there was no progress. A steady file of well-wishers saw to that.

They formed into a mob, and before he knew what was happening he was airborne again – this time off the end of the pier and into the harbour. The competitors, in traditional style, celebrated the victory and with it the end of a memorable week of racing.

Breaking the surface, Richard spluttered seawater for the second time. 'Jonny doesn't know what he's missing,' he said, and struck out along the harbour wall, heading for shore. After a few strokes of an awkward crawl he instead opted for a leisurely float on his back. He relished the moment. On cue, the Devon sun broke through the late afternoon chill. Richard was at peace with the world. The fleet looked on, and their applause was music to his ears.

Chapter Seventeen

Ultimate Debriefing

Jonny had returned the hero. Arm in sling but nothing broken or detached.

'Just a nasty shoulder strain – bloody sore though. Never mind, I'm sure I'll be able to lift my trophy tonight.' He played down his injury, but his point was modestly made. The focus, for the moment, was on the delivery of two pints. With his good hand he had carried them from the marquee. Samantha and Penny, having deposited him outside the club, had more important things on their minds. More important, at any rate, than listening to yet another re-run of the days battles and jousts.

Richard was equally inattentive. He was in reflective mood.

'Cheers mate. Good to see you fit and well again. Well, at least smiling.' He assisted him with the descent, down onto the grass. The landing in spite of Richard's caring side, was bumpy; a jolt of pain and some spillage. Sympathy, however, was in short supply because Richard, leaning on one elbow and taking a generous sip, said simply: 'Lager?'

'Too hot for beer – just drink and enjoy.' Richard, Jonny realised, was preparing to launch into his overview of the week's proceedings – and Jonny was already looking for an escape route.

'You know Jonny, this is that funny old time. You know, between the end of a regatta and the prize giving; purgatory perhaps. The adrenalin has evaporated from each and every pore of your bruised body. You just want to lay back and sleep, but the old brain is gearing up for celebrations ahead. You hear what I'm saying, mate?'

Jonny nodded wisely, and paused before replying.

'Hey – heavy stuff mate. You on pills too?'

Richard wasn't receiving. With pint tankard in hand, soon to be replaced by a magnificent silver cup, the sun beating down on his matted salt-encrusted hair, he remained within the world of D'Arcy. His monologue had continued seamlessly. Jonny had stretched out on the grass, his arm crossed over his chest, his lager parked by his side. Eyelids heavy, he was listening; a little.

'Jonny boy, we left the beach this morning like a couple of gladiators, and returned victorious, albeit like two rather washed-up

Vikings. Look at us. Me, covered in plasters and tholing a cracking headache; you, ghostly, bruised and all trussed up. Ah, the price of fame, eh?' There was no diverting him from his train of thought.

'I don't know what you think, but there's just something about a championship week that is uncannily sociable.' His train rolled on. 'People with whom you have little or nothing in common just merge and mingle. It's entirely different from the 'Spanish holiday' syndrome. Okay, you fly out to the baking sun. You hit it off, maybe even get laid a few times, and then... nothing – or at best, vague memories filed away in a photograph album.'

He had unwittingly opened the debriefing book again. 'Could you,' he concluded, 'have imagined a better holiday than this?'

'Yeah, I see what you mean, man.' Jonny tried to get a word in. 'Take those O'Brien brothers for example. Never seen or heard of them before, but in an instant a relationship was sparked.' He looked thoughtful. 'I'm sure, Rich, that like me you were a bit conscious of being a Brit. You know, an English bloke in their company. I mean, considering the mayhem in Ireland – what we see on the box every night.'

'Yeah. Soldiers, explosions, images of a country at war.'

'I was amazed to learn that people over there lead normal lives, never mind being able to go sailing.'

'Didn't we have great craic with them though? Bloody hell, I'm even talking like them. One thing I did notice though – you see how slick they were at diverting questions when we probed a little too deeply at times?'

'As you mention it, I did, but don't forget they had just escaped from their troubled enclave for a few days. You can understand why they politely put up the barriers. By the way, are you serious about accepting their invitation? Would you travel over there?'

'I would,' said Richard. 'I wasn't up for it at first, I was just being polite, but I am now.'

'What changed your mind?' Jonny looked serious.

'It was something Eoin said. Do you remember? Something like, "Look boys, we can't deny that there are shadowy figures lurking in dark places, that bad things don't happen back home. But please don't take everything you see on a TV screen as absolute fact." He also said that if a camera was taken back ten feet, what was portrayed as a serious riot would often be seen for what it was; a fekkin good brawl on a street corner. Then when he knew I was coming round to the idea, he suggested that their catholic verses protestant troubles were not that dissimilar to ours. He was talking about something universal – the mixed-race quandary. At first I was puzzled, but he pointed out that the combination of John Tyndall and his National Front mobs, against the emerging Black Panther sympathy groups would become *our* British tinderbox. I just nodded – he clearly knew more about us Brits than I did about the Irish.'

'And?' Jonny was intrigued.

'Then he asked me straight out. He said, "sure, come over to us... for a wee break in the tranquillity of an Ulster Lough".'

Richard shrugged, his palms outstretched in front of him. 'How could I have refused?'

Jonny, his painkillers wearing off, considered himself to be back on planet reality. He challenged Richard.

'Bloody hell Rich, we've got ourselves into a deep old chasm here. Crikey, we're talking sailing adventures, not about making the world a better place.'

Richard, however, was on his own parade.

'Mate, I'm deadly serious. I mean, it would just be a few hours of driving up to Stranraer, and Larne Lough is where the ferry actually docks.' He looked at Jonny. 'So how's about it Jonny boy? Fancy joining me in the Emerald Isle next year?'

'Okay by me skipper. I suppose. Better run it past the folks first.' He didn't sound convinced.

'Never thought of that – ah, it'll be okay, they'll be find with it.'

'It's a no-brainer, I suppose.' Jonny was gravely nodding, statesmanlike, but slipped in a tiny barb: 'Depends on timing, and how brave you are.'

Richard's overview widened into gossip and tittle-tattle. Jonny had discovered mid-week, that Eoin was studying dentistry at Queens University in Belfast. He and Eoin would get on famously. Fergal was a maths teacher, which, Jonny assumed, was why he and the crazy Hayley obviously clicked.

'The thought of her teaching kids sums still blows me away,' added Jonny, before turning his attention to the Scots.

'So...what's your general view on Ewan and Alison?'

'Ay-e, the Scots. You tell me.'

Jonny said: 'Well, thought she was a bit butch, but attractive. I mean, wouldn't have kicked her out of the bunk.'

'Bloody hell Jonny; and you under the spell of the lovely Penny. Anything you want to talk about, in confidence like, Jonny boy?'

'Piss off, you know what I mean,' he said, but Richard caught a little flush. 'I actually thought that she and Ewan were an item already.'

'No, she let it slip that she had split up with her bloke, an accountant, a few weeks before coming down here. He was a fair bit older than her; she said that after several years together they had little in common.

'That,' said Jonny, 'explains a lot. Touchy-feely, a bit of a tease, and that in-your-face, fancy a flirt act. A bit too convivial, a bit over-sociable. Know something Rich? I reckon it was she who was dumped. So this week our Alison was very much on the rebound. She'd been on the lookout for a revenge shag.'

'Don't you be hangin back there Jonny boy' He paused deliberately, then questioned. 'Are you, by any chance, saying that you made a move on her and were rejected? Remember Jonny boy, the week's not over yet.'

He got the look again.

'Ewan, now he was a really interesting guy with a twang I could listen to for ages.' Jonny shifted onto his good elbow. He looked uncomfortable, his shoulder obviously giving him jip. The remains of the lager was flat and warm. But he continued with his drift;

'His told me his main job was a Clyde pilot. But interestingly, he also spends periods helping his old man. He is, or was, a delivery skipper. He rattled off an atlas of places they brought big boats back from.' He was obviously impressed. 'Imagine spending a summer playing with rich boys' toys and getting paid!' Richard was engrossed. Jonny continued: 'Some of his tales were hair-raising. He described incidents in gale after gale, and some of the scraps he got into around Glasgow after dark. It made me shiver. You would get on well with him.'

Jonny had decided not to allow Richard's midweek skirmish to be brushed under anyone's carpet. He realised that the tale could be pulled out, polished up and further embellished whenever necessary, especially if Richard was in danger of getting big headed. Which undoubtedly he would be.

'Very funny.'

If Jonny thought he had got the last word, Richard had other ideas. He continued to roll out opinions, covering one by one the personalities they had encountered during that wonderful August week.

'Darren Brett and Herbie Martin. A bit stand-offish. I've nodded at them at other regattas but on the Wednesday I actually got a conversation out of them. Good blokes, a bit posh.'

Jonny said: 'That Darren fella, he's in the same game as you, isn't he?'

'Yeah, different industry – plastics – and a bit more senior,' said Richard. 'Way ahead of you this time Jonny.' Actually I felt a bit guilty picking his brains the other day. But then again I have a new challenge to go home to. So any extra assistance is invaluable; we exchanged addresses and business cards. That's what you do in business, but you medics wouldn't understand...'

Jonny didn't take the bait. Instead, he deferred to Richard as the self appointed chair of the analysing committee.

'Overall, the social side was the best ever, certainly blew last year away.'

'Après sail? Brilliant, I agree –best ever. What about the gangly Isherwood twins – identical or what! I never really knew whether I was talking to James or John until they were afloat; John was always at the helm. Cut a fine dash, though, in all that matching gear, especially afloat. They looked cool.'

'Didn't really take to them,' said Richard. 'I was polite though.' Jonny took over;

'Thought they were mostly up their own asses, truth be told.' 'Now don't you be holding back, mate.' Richard was again taken aback by Jonny's acid comments. 'I kind of agree though. I think most of us believe that there was a bit of mischief in that pair. Wonder what they made of us? Hayley wondered if they swapped girlfriends. I suggested she was out of order, but at the same time she planted the seed, and I must admit it lingers.'

Jonny couldn't resist.

'Well at least something's growing in there, other than lust for the gorgeous Samantha.'

Richard choose not to answer – he was learning. He continued: 'They hail from the Anglesey direction. Regular regatta goers, and making their way steadily up the rankings like ourselves. Dave Gilmore reckoned that this would be their last championship week – said they were determined to make their mark before going high performance, and maybe even an Olympic campaign'

As for the Steve's, Marsden and Staunton, from the Solent, neither Richard nor Jonny, nor indeed Dave had ever got to know them beyond a polite nod. They always seemed to drift away after each evening's prize giving, regardless of where a regatta was held. Andy Smith, from the same club, made up for them though – on that they agreed. He was the stereotypical London East End boy. He had a story for every occasion. He too was doing his last championship. He had moved into offshore yachts and his crewman Francis (Fran) O'Reilly was moving lock, stock and barrel to the States, apparently to take up a position at a Florida University. Andy, underneath his rugged exterior, was a sales director for a big retail chain. Richard had also discovered that he held a first class honours degree in economics. Never judge a book by its cover, he thought.

As they talked on about newly kindled friendships, Richard suddenly had a 'middle of the night' moment.

'Shit Jonny, I completely forgot to say.'

'All right little man, calm down, calm down – you haven't got Samantha pregnant already?'

'Very droll.' That was the best he could manage on the spur of the moment. He forged on: 'No, listen, this is important. Remember the Wilsons, Rodger & Gwen, who got that second place in Thursday's race?' Jonny nodded. 'Well, they are, it seems, so enthused by the whole affair that they want first refusal on our mistress.'

'I didn't know she was for sale,' said Jonny.

'No, nor me either .I've never been a situation like this. Apparently it's not unusual for the top boats to be sold on at the end of a national regatta. And make no mistake mate, we do have the top boat. I'm thinking that if we could get a decent price for her we might be able to put a successful bid together for the Gilmore boat – which, I'm fairly sure, will be fully repaired and on the market as soon as Michael delivers his news to Dave.'

'News? What news? Rich, it's like living in a parallel universe around you at times.'

'Remember the night that Dave got completely slaughtered?'

'Which particular night ... okay, okay, go on.'

'I'm trying to, mate. Well, not long after, Michael cornered me and spurted out the whole sorry Dave tale, confiding in me that he was intent on splitting up their partnership after this event – I promised him I wouldn't breathe a word, and I didn't.'

'Oh, okay, that's fair enough I suppose,' agreed Jonny .'Thanks for telling me anyway. Clearly the secret won't go to the grave with you, then.'

'Fair comment – I'll tell you more when we get home, okay? At any rate, you see where my devious little mind is taking us. But only if you're on board.'

Jonny went into one of his 'quiet moments'. I swear he does it for badness, just to rile me, Richard thought.

'Yep — I'm on board. Their boat really is like a piece of Chippendale furniture.' There was a note of youthful excitement in his voice.

'Actually it is; it was built by Chippendales. Jack Chippendale, the Norfolk boat builder.'

After that remark, Richard felt somewhere between smug and smart arse. The conversation paused.

'Right, I'm off for that shower, and to get rid of this sling for at least a moment.'

'Do you need me to wash you down...pet?' teased Richard. Jonny didn't answer, just shook his head and proceeded to the wash rooms.

'Okay, catch you back at the van,' called Richard.

And with that, he was on his own again, and reminiscing. Although this was only their second full championship week they were totally smitten, already confirmed for the following year. Richard allowed his thoughts to race ahead to next season, and the scenario of a title defence without his trusty crewman. He figured that Jonny would be qualified soon, and by the time the championship came around God only knows where he'd be practicing, or living for that matter. Their friendship, notwithstanding, was rock solid even though of late they tended to mix in differing circles.

They came from different sides of the track. Jonny was Mr Academia and Richard, well he was hauling himself, albeit with growing momentum, up from the shop floor. There were times when the boys' worlds fractured and unravelled. Generally though, their nautical and musical bonds were strong enough to avoid lasting damage.

In truth, Richard harboured a niggling regret at not making it to university himself. In his rise up industry's ranks his failure to engage academically allowed feelings of insecurity to knock his confidence; for example, when working alongside fast-tracking graduates or when engaged in conversation with 'posh types', some of whom were Jonny's peers.

Such was the developing scenario as he prepared to meet the potential purchasers of their mistress. Posh? Yes, Gwen, and especially Roger Wilson, were posh personified.

Richard had slipped into pensive mood. Was he perhaps being a little too self-critical for his own good? If so, it was hardly the moment. But he had met so many great people that week; all types and all classes. He and Jonny had been invited to guest at so many clubs and functions around the country. Other than the defence of their own title, however, only one event was confirmed: the O'Brien's Irish outing. And now, with Jonny's approval secured, it was time for Richard to chase up that potential offer on *Satisfaction*.

He spied the Wilsons, gazing bleary eyed at his soon-to-be ex-mistress. He drew in the biggest breath his lungs would allow. His heart rate slowed. *Let's not get ahead of ourselves, Richard.* He tightened his reins. Remember son, he told himself: remember how they goad you back at the office – *buyers make the worst sellers.* These were uncharted waters. The sale of his previous dinghy didn't count; in truth she had sold herself and there wasn't much money involved. He was apprehensive, but he had a plan.

The stroll, and it was a stroll, down to his mistress and her admirers, was slow but deliberate. He had to prepare himself. Yes they were posh, but he was the national champion. They wanted something that he had.

The last three steps. *Right Richard, smile. Shoulders back – you can do this – one more deep breath.* His arm was already outstretched...

Chapter Eighteen

The Ex-mistress

'Well, hello again – you must be really pleased with your week, Gwen'. Richard, his best diction on display, tentatively approached the curious couple. 'So, where did you eventually finish in the placings?'

'Twenty-eighth,' she replied. 'Best ever result at a nationals and best in the club too. And gosh, Roger and I have had the most wonderful week of sailing, darling.'

Roger interjected: 'Jolly great sport, eh? You chaps really left it to the last moment. I mean, how did you *do* it?'

Richard sensed a sales opening.

'It helps if you have the right equipment.'

His first clumsy attempt at a sales pitch had fallen, he felt, on deaf ears. He returned to polite conversation, thinking, *I'll never mock those sales lads again...*

'You must be over the moon, Roger,' he said. But he couldn't help himself; without waiting for a reply, he went in for the kill:

'Are you still interested in our little star here?'

Gwen answered for her husband, who appeared to have been somewhat sidelined.

'Yes indeed we are, Richard,' she said, and without further preamble she went on to pose, without taking breath, *the key* question:

'How much are you asking for her, darling?'

'Well, to be honest...' Richard, now facing them square-on, attempted to throttle Gwen back to a more manageable pace. He was trying to establish a firm negotiating platform: one that hopefully favoured his position. His hand was stroking his jaw; his head was bowed. He finally spoke.

'I, em — I don't really know.' As he pulled at his lower lip with thumb and forefinger, another manufactured pause was created. He, himself, recalled in that moment, one particular character, a commercial traveller who frequently negotiated with him. The man would go into a similar routine at the first hint of a buying signal.

'You see, Gwen, my problem is that I've had a hell of a time trying to persuade my partner that we should actually let her go at all.' Almost in unison their faces dropped to the floor. Negotiations had stalled, but Richard felt that he had a measure of control. He let the moment hang, then quickly re-established the mood and quelled any sense of awkwardness.

'He did eventually agree,' he said, 'but on the understanding that she goes to a good home.' Now he was even embarrassing himself with his patter, but he continued undaunted. 'The work that Jonny put into this boat was amazing, so I can fully understand his reluctance.'

He had learnt a few of the tricks over the years.

'We understand.'

The Wilsons nodded politely, but in an unexpected and rather assertive interruption Roger asked: 'Is she for sale, or not, young fellow?'

This brought an unanticipated pause in negotiations; control had shifted. Richard swayed uneasily from foot to foot. A give-away. He was rattled. His initial sureness had taken a bit of a knock– this selling lark was not as easy as he had begun to believe. However, he quickly composed himself. Roger, he could see, was no amateur – he knew exactly what Richard was up to.

His palms were moist. He could feel the heat rising up his neck, but he wasn't going to let his old insecurities spoil his day. He stuck to his sales plan, and with renewed confidence mustered a reply.

'Er...yes. Yes, I can confirm that *Satisfaction*, or as she was once known, *Kittiwake*, is indeed for sale, and that Jonny and I would be delighted to consider an offer from your good selves. His tactic –

again he'd noted various sales guys' techniques – was not to put a straight price on the valued mistress's head. Rather, put her up for auction.

This might well realise a return above the market rate. He had gambled. An offer was duly made. He nearly wet himself, digging deep to retain a cool facade. What he really wanted to do was jump two feet in the air and shout halleluiah, but somehow he returned to the selling doctrine that his colleague, the company's sales director, preached: 'If the buying signal is positive and an offer acceptable – shut up; don't say another word. Don't break the spell!'

And that's exactly what he did. After what seemed like an age – like, he thought, one of Jonny's interminable thinking moments – he declared: 'Mr and Mrs Wilson, you've got yourself a deal. Look after her, please.'

He got a big wet smacker right on the cheek from Gwen and a simultaneous enthusiastic handshake from Roger. Roger gave Gwen a celebration embrace. A very satisfactory result all round. It occurred to Richard that Gwen wouldn't need to salt her chips tonight, after the layer of Torbay crud she had just removed from his cheek.

They agreed to reconvene on Saturday, and conclude the business element of the transaction; 2 p.m. was the agreed time. Roger passed over his telephone number in case any changes occurred. They shook again and Richard declared:

'Look, I'm off to clean up – git rid of this salt. We'll meet up later for a celebratory G&T, okay?' Listen to me, he thought; if I spend any more time down here I'm going to turn posh.

He decided that he liked the Wilsons.

'Excellent idea', they agreed. Then they all went their separate ways, everyone smiling broadly. Gwen, however, stopped and turned.

'Richard darling, do you think Jonny would be annoyed if we changed the colour scheme?'

'Oh Gwen,' he smiled, 'colour is such a personal thing; as *Kittiwake* she was an embarrassing orange. You must refashion and rebrand her for her new life just as you wish. No, Jonny will not be annoyed in the slightest. 'Richard got another hug – no kiss this time. Finally they parted company. He felt like doing an Eric Morecambe sidekick, but then thought better of it, telling himself to remain cool – to act, in fact, like an adult. His next thought was on the whereabouts of Jonny; he needed to celebrate too!

Chapter Nineteen

1:Towards the Night

Richard had remained in a funny old mood. He didn't know whether it was the sapping effect of the day, the rollercoaster of the race itself, the elation/despair/elation of the finish, or indeed the non-stop flow of well-wishers. But he was definitely feeling a bit grumpy and sour. Even his dad questioned his form when he telegraphed through the news. It wasn't that he was fed-up or depressed. How could he be? He'd just won *the* national championship and simultaneously met the most wonderful, beautiful creature on this earth. Plus, he had sold a boat for a tidy sum. A touch of sunstroke? Maybe. Then he thought again, and his catholic upbringing prompted a question:

I wonder: is this really purgatory?

Regardless, he was glad of a bit of quiet time to himself. If nothing else, it might stop his head spinning and throbbing. He had declined Penny and Jonny's kind invitation to join them for a steak Diane and a glass or two of Blue Nun; opting, instead, for the delights of the local chippie. Anyway, as Samantha was back up in Torquay, he wasn't in any mood to play chaperone.

What is it, he thought, about fish and chips straight out of the paper?

His stroll along the esplanade had done the trick. It was probably hunger, or nervous exhaustion, which had made him such a party-pooper. He hadn't eaten since breakfast; he popped into another shop for a Kit Kat and a Coke, thinking: *Need to keep the bunkers well filled. There'll be a lot of liquid to soak up later.*

He wandered back to the campsite. After a doze, his energy levels were restored, but on departure a glimpse of his reflected profile in the VW window suggested – ordered – a complete fashion change. He also treated himself to a cold-water shave, wishing he'd done so after showering when his skin was soft – ouch!

After applying the Old Spice (ouch! again) he replaced the plasters with somewhat neater strips. He also noticed that he would soon be sporting a glorious shiner. Refreshed and re-fashioned, he was finally ready to rock and roll.

'Right, okay, lead me into the limelight. I'm ready to face up to my new national status,' he declared aloud – then looked around to see if anyone might have overheard. He agreed with himself that he was dressed to kill. Resplendent in new brown platforms over which pale green flares were fetchingly draped. A royal blue satin shirt – three buttons open – fought with a greenish cord jacket. He reckoned that he was fit and ready to receive the cup. Then, preparing to pull back the awning to expose himself to the waiting world, he hesitated. *Would Samantha just see him in the same light?* Perhaps, he thought, his chosen garb was the prelude to sartorial suicide…

'Yeah,' he said aloud, 'far too much going on. Too much Julian: not enough Richard.' He returned to the suitcases, declaring that there *was* a time when you could actually make a firm fashion decision for yourself. Then he thought, is this what love does to a chap?

So finally he was changed. This was it – the final get-up. A dark blue, ever so slightly creased linen suit sat perfectly with the paisley patterned shirt; white collar out over the jacket. He kept the shoes but dropped the pocket handkerchief. On close inspection he reckoned he looked pretty cool. He was ready to meet his public. Though mildly concerned about the eye, he casually brushed the issue aside. *It doesn't look too good, but that's for Sam to sort out. I mean it's either going to be a medical or a make-up solution in advance of the photo calls.*

Strutting into the marquee, he was almost brought up short. Yes, it was early evening, but other than the club volunteers setting out the prizes, the bar staff re-stocking and a few other members tidying, the bloody tent was deserted.

He wandered around aimlessly. He acknowledged a man whom he assumed was an electrician. He was up a ladder high over the stage area. Nodding, he watched for a few moments, waved briefly, cast another eye around the cavernous reaches of the big tent, and strolled away.

'Shit, what do I do now?' he mumbled to himself. Before progressing in the general direction of clubhouse bar, Richard veered left, stopping opposite the display of prizes. He focused on the magnificent silver cup. He paused, swallowed hard, drew in a gasp of air.

'Ah, the sweet smell of success – Brasso.' This time he wasn't in the least concerned if anyone had heard him. After all, he was the champion, the national champion of the UK and beyond!

'Richard. I say, you're looking a bit dapper this evening.' It was Gwen, bouncing in his direction. She planted another of her juicy kisses on his forehead, avoiding his puffed-up cheek...

'You're looking lovely Gwen. And the old man cleans up well too,' he said, nodding at Roger. Gwen went off into one of her infectious laughing spasms.

'Right you two, its G&T time,' Richard announced, directing them to a corner alcove.

Richard ordered drinks at the bar.

'Cheers, and health to sail.' They clinked glasses. Their table was dressed with a navy cloth, and a central vase of purple pansies. Two fizzing G&Ts were delivered; Gwen had opted for a Pimms. Richard had also ordered one for Penny, as she and Jonny were due at any moment. He wasn't sure what his mate would be drinking. Penny had acquired a taste for the Pimms since her arrival on Thursday. Neither he nor Jonny were too fussed on it, even though the company had sponsored one of the races that week. Gwen had turned her attention to Richard.

'Oh Richard dear, that eye of yours is looking a bit colourful. Is it painful?' She was now standing leaning over him, inspecting the damage. She was well aware where Richard's eyes were focused...

'Only when I laugh,' was the smug reply. But if he was honest it was bloody sore.

Richard sort of suspected that Gwen was in medicine. Roger had just sold off his pharmacy business; he was enjoying his new-found leisure time and 'fortune'. So was Richard – any earlier qualms about the amount they paid for *Satisfaction* had been long since been smothered.

They were soon joined by Penny and Jonny. Richard did the introductions. Jonny went for the gin option. Gwen was on her feet faster than Richard over the side of the boat. She was all over Jonny like a rash – all boat talk of course. Penny glanced at Richard, her eyes narrow. Richard just winked and smiled back; he leant over and whispered to her.

'Call it after-sales, Penn.'

She smiled thinly. Jonny was sharing Richard's interest in bosoms. Penny, as Richard had noticed, was not impressed. A covert tap on his mate's ankle alerted him to the brewing squall, and any further fall-out was averted. Conversation flowed, the deal had been secured and the time for the handover reset. Before they realised, it was prize giving time.

With the natural light rapidly fading it became clear that the tent had been dramatically transformed from the weekly mustering station into an environment fit for any top-end awards ceremony. Richard felt those butterflies again – or was it the tonic…

Oh, I wish Samantha could have been here… Bloody hospital.

2: Prize Giving and Awards Ceremony

The MC, also the event chairman, had now presented himself in formal attire; reefer replaced with black tie. However, for Richard, he was still the wee fat man, with big specs and booming vocals.

'Ladies and gen-tle-men, boys and girls and special guests; welcome to this the final celebration of your championship week...'

Prize giving's were always the bane of Richard D'Arcy's boating life. It wasn't that he disliked receiving trophies regardless of how ugly some of them were. No, it was all the faffing around and the awful speeches. Putting it all together they just reeked of make-do amateurism. Most ceremonies rolled on for far too long. They frequently ate into precious drive-home time. They irritated him. Tonight, however, Richard sensed it was definitely going to be different. 'Lavish' would have done it a disservice; the marquee had been completely revamped. It seemed to have acquired an inner skin; been transformed into a west end stage setting that literally took his breath away. How did they do it, Richard thought, and in such a short time? A couple of hours ago it was a tent. He turned, nudged his mate.

'What do you think of this set-up then, Jonny boy?'

'It's almost like one of those awards do's. Is this all for us?'.

'Yeah, let's hold that thought – why are you always right about things?' Richard's tongue once again firmly back in his cheek.

'Crikey, I can even hear what that guy up there is saying.'

'Well then, shut up and listen,' tutted Penny. *Oh – get her.* End of conversation. Richard's thoughts drifted back to Samantha. What on earth could be keeping her away until this time? How long can you spend healing the sick, for goodness sake?

I need you here pet. I need your support. I just want to impress you. Is that asking too much?

He looked up to the ceiling. *Always late.* He was getting himself into a right old Richard state.

By the time Richard's attention had drifted back to the stage, the MC had introduced himself to the throng and explained, step by step, how the ceremony would play out. Then, after a short pause for dramatic effect, he introduced representatives of each day's sponsoring company. There were six of them. 'After this section,' he continued, 'we will present on your behalf a number of special awards to key personnel who have organised and run this national championship. Then, the show will move onto the main event, the presentation of overall prizes.'

As he stretched his left arm towards the table a cheer filled the marquee. Richard had picked up on the word 'show', for indeed that was what it was. He hoped, however, that it wouldn't become a drama, at least not for him. Not yet finished, the MC announced that these prizes would start at tenth place overall and, in reverse order, would lead up to the ultimate, the national award: the magnificent sterling silver championship cup.

'That's us mate, that's us, you and me!' Richard again nudged Jonny, unable to contain his excitement. Jonny, however, was cool as a cucumber – outwardly at least. He placed his good arm on Richard's shoulder and nodded in agreement. Richard looked at him and thought: *You really are a bit cool. Hope you've got a decent speech written, ya big git.*

Jonny did all the speeches – he was just one of those guys who was gifted. He had a natural ability to articulate, and Richard hadn't; he was always happy to take a back seat.

The MC paused in his reprise. It was just long enough for a hush to descend. Then, with all the theatre he could muster, his arms stretched wide, he commanded:

'LETS – GET – ON – WITH – THE – SHOW!'

The lights in the main body of the marquee dimmed as music filled the stage. Jonny was first to recognise it as 'The Ride of the Valkyries'. He couldn't resist a glance skywards. The drama was indeed building. The boys were fascinated, captivated. While the show gathered momentum, Richard's excitement was starting to turn to mild frustration. Everyone, it seemed, except the champions was getting a prize. That was, of course, until this opening phase of the evening's schedule had wound its way to the winners of the final race of the series. Now it was their time.

'Ladies & gentlemen, please welcome Mrs Frankie Dalrymple, managing director of the Royal Hotel Group, our sponsors for the final race of your championship.' He continued seamlessly: 'The winners of this race – it was probably the most exciting finish of any series – are of course…' (big pause). Get on with it mouthed Penny.

'RICHARD D'ARCY and JONNY DUBOIS, from…'

Richard led the way to the podium. But amid the applause and back-slapping, a lonely tear of sadness had welled up within him. He had so wished that Samantha could have been witness to this occasion. The trophy before him was actually quite beautiful; a special piece, a brand new trophy, it was sculpted in silver plate on teak and ash. It depicted sails on a wave-crested sea. Mrs Dalrymple was tall and stylish, classically dressed in a black halter-neck knee length dress accessorised with an array of jewellery which was competing with the trophy. Richard reckoned that she was in her mid-forties; *great legs*. For her trouble she received two boyish pecks on her cheek as she passed over the trophy. Suddenly, Richard felt quite alone up there. But he focused on Penny, who was waving and wolf-whistling. Then he presented the trophy to their adoring fans, raising it above his head to enthusiastic cheers. A micro-shred of jealousy was directed towards Jonny – he was indeed missing Sam.

Strolling back to the floor, Jonny said casually, 'What on earth must she have thought, approached on one flank by you, with your coloured-in eye and those plasters, and on the other by me in this flamin sling?' They just looked at each other and smiled. Back at their table the trophy was placed safely in Penny's care.

The various special awards efficiently followed. Then it was on to the main part of the evening. As the lights dimmed, 'The Ride of the Valkyries' was again faded up. This fanfare was accompanied by a flashing cascade of coloured spotlights. The decibel level rose higher. Neither Richard nor Jonny had ever seen such a performance, certainly not at a sailing event. Jonny turned to Richard and said to him quietly:

'Crikey, I hope my speech is okay? It's all getting a bit manic and showbiz up there. You may have to hold my hand, mate.'

Richard was momentarily catapulted into shock. Jonny was, he sensed, crapping himself!

Ah, sure my Jonny boy will be okay – you better be mate, 'cos I've not prepared anything.

The MC had now started his run-through to the finish; this was the culmination of not only six gruelling races for the D'Arcy-Dubois sailboat team, but the final moments of Richard's five-year dream.

'In tenth place overall ladies and gents, let's hear it for…'

'Miss HAYLEY HARTLEY-SMYTH and ROBIN HAYES.

'In ninth place – PAUL OWEN and Miss LAURA GRAHAM '

As the tension continued to mount, neither Richard nor Jonny – nor, for that matter, Penny – would recall who took the various other overall places. Well, other than those claimed by their club mates Alan Burton and Patrick Duffy, in sixth place overall, and of course Paul and Laura too. All in all it was a great showing from their club. Their combined concentration was however focused on their fast approaching moment in the spotlight; their time was getting ever closer. Richard, fidgeting, looked around in the vain hope that Samantha would, just in time, come gliding to his side.

'And... in third place – the 'Steve's' he paused again, then announced at even higher volume, 'it's STEPHEN MARSDEN AND STEVEN STAUNTON, from across there,' he pointed, 'in the Solent.'

The ceremony had moved along with great fluidity, as each of the recipients entered and exited the stage. Richard turned to Jonny, talking over the MC's next pronouncement;

'Jeez, mate this is a slick operation, if not a bit....' he was stopped in mid sentence.

'The runners-up in this year's championship, *another* southern team; 'ANDREW SMITH and FRANCIS O'REILLY, also from the Solent.' And suddenly the stage was bare, and laid bare too, in both boy's eyes was something of a southern bias in the MC's delivery. They smiled a contented smile at each other; they knew each other.

Only two trophies and a dramatic floral display remained on the stylishly dressed table. The show had reached its finale. This was the moment the capacity crowd had been waiting for; anticipation gripped the marquee and a hush gradually extended over the audience; the tinkle of glassware was silenced. The air of excitement was triggered as new theme music faded up. Richard was instantly aware that it was Booker T's *Green Onions.* Smiling, he felt a lump swelling in his throat. Simultaneously the decibel and luminary levels increased. Spontaneous applause and a rhythmic clap waved its way towards the frontage.

The stage had itself been bathed, first in blue, then red and finally white. The MC again rose from his position beside the prize table. A single spotlight followed him as he swaggered back to his lectern. His final sequence of announcements followed; he was in his element.

'Ladies and gentlemen, members, competitors and guests. Please welcome your commodore, Mr Roland Chisholme, and his daughter Samantha, to present your new champions with their hard-fought-for winnings.' The spotlight found new subjects.

Father and daughter emerged from a side awning into the limelight. As the audience rose to their feet, Richard stiffened. He gripped his partner's forearm. Jonny winced. Richard's complexion had noticeably paled. He was trembling. Jonny, aware that his partner could well be on the verge of fainting, released his grip, then quickly swapped places to clasp him round the waist with his good arm. He shook him and said quietly:

'Come on mate, deep breath. You've left me once already today; can't afford another early departure.' Penny, now aware of the developing scenario, moved to Richard's side to render extra support. Richard finally spoke, albeit with a tremor in his voice.

'But, but she's— the commodore's daughter! Jonny, Penn; did you know this? DID YOU KNOW?' Richard stuttered and gasped. Penny looked away, a trifle embarrassed. She was also hiding a wry smile as she fiddled with her hand bag and the remains of her Pimms. Jonny held station, supporting his skipper. Richard just stood there hypnotised, gazing at the stage and his mysterious Samantha. Penny stole a glance, and smiled as Jonny answered;

'You mean – *you* didn't?' Jonny looked at his skipper in semi disbelief. He had himself just discovered the connection from Penny that afternoon. She, of course, had assumed all along that the boys, especially Richard, knew exactly who they were dealing with; it is indeed, she thought to herself, a self-centred man's world, God help us! Predictably, Richard didn't really hear the opening sentence of the announcement and introduction.

'So finally everyone, here they are, your 1975 national champions.' Big pause.

'RICHARD D'ARCY and Mr JONATHAN DUBOIS! Let's hear it for them!'

The music boomed. The seams of the marquee must have been fully stressed by the accompanying explosion of sound, of cheering and of applause. They had won the title and the popular vote. They just looked at each other for what seemed like a lifetime. They absorbed the adulation. It finally had hit home. This was it: confirmation, if confirmation were needed after today's incredible charge to the finish, that they were the best!

Number One! Certainly for Penny and Samantha, Roland and Henry – Hilary was not present.

As Jonny moved Richard towards the stage he realised that they were going nowhere. Ring-leaders Dave and Michael, together with the Isherwood twins, had grasped both of their belts, thus preventing them, in nautical tradition, from stepping onto the long road to the podium. The crowd were in hysterics. This intervention conveniently allowed Richard to regain at least a modicum of composure. He continued to berate himself. He was breathing deeply; he had to regain control. At last, his heartbeat was slowing.

The commodore's daughter. How did I not realise? And sister to those flaming Chisholme brothers – man, I'm so slow. He continued to interrogate himself. *What am I going to say...?* Richard was now ready. He was as ready as he'd ever be for this, his victorious journey; but as the walk – at funeral pace – progressed, another veil, a veil of embarrassment, draped itself around him. His immaturity, his infamous skeletons – they were stirring again.

It had all been staring him in the face, and he hadn't picked up on a single thread of it. All week he had been so engrossed in competition and his own well-being, that he never so much as focused a blink on anything or anyone else, except Jonny. He was now suffering the consequences. It was as if a short sharp penance had been asked of him. He was mortified. *What a complete blind idiot I am. Good God I never even...what a dickhead! What am I going to say to her? She's not stupid, she'll know. I don't believe this is happening!*

As he navigated the three steps onto the stage, Richard's eyes locked onto Samantha's. She was a vision, stunning, in a deep purple satin figure-hugging strapless dress. 'Wow,' he mouthed to her. Roland moved forward to shake their hands, and he quietly said to Richard:

'Well done, my boy, had total confidence, as had the daughter.' He then turned and warmly shook Jonny's hand, ushering him towards Samantha. She presented him with his personal trophy – a maple and mahogany shield engraved with all the previous winning crews' names. An embrace and a cheek-to-cheek kiss followed. Jonny and Samantha then stepped back and to one side.

As the MC called for Richard to lift the championship trophy, it finally got to him. Tears welled. They trickled around his swollen eye socket and onto his cheeks. It stung, and he blinked hard. He carried on, somewhat unsteadily. Jonny, however, was totally focused on the developing scenario. As his skipper accepted the champion's cup from Samantha, she leaned in closer to him and within her embrace she whispered in his ear.

'This is only the beginning Richard, I love you babe.'

The next thing Richard heard was a sound akin to those starting cannons. Jonny, foreseeing disaster, was off at speed on a closing tack. 'Shit,' he gasped, 'I don't believe it. He's dropped the bloody trophy!'

Without any fuss, he glided onto the target like an outfield player. One-handed, he had the monster cup's base rescued. The crowd responded with a huge cheer. Samantha, meanwhile, had placed a second kiss just below Richard's tender closing eye – he felt no pain.

Further drama skilfully averted, Jonny stepped up to the microphone, true to form. Like a holy man calming the seas, resplendent in a white linen suit setting off a petrol blue embroidered shirt, three buttons open, its collar obscured by his shoulder-length hair, he raised his hand. The crowd fell silent. He opened with his usual panache.

Richard had retired two paces back– Samantha too. Her right arm was draped around Richard's waist, her hand gripping his belt. She knew her boy was still a bit shaky. He, however, had other issues on his mind. Jonny was not his usual Mr Cool. This ratcheted the tension; then there was that background music, the decibels now drastically reduced. Another favourite by Booker T: *Time Is Tight.* Richard was a massive fan. Frowning, he began to wonder: was this music specially chosen as a final prize for the new champion? Little did he realise that indeed it had been. The commodore's daughter could be a tad devious when the situation demanded...

'Lord Mayor.' Jonny turned to his left. 'Commodore.' He faced the audience again. 'Principal Race Officer, Mr Lockett, ladies and gentlemen, distinguished guests, our sponsors, and of course you, our fellow competitors. What I have to say won't take long.'

At this point a Selotaped cascade of A5 paper unfolded itself. It descended from his free hand to the stage floor to great laughter and spontaneous applause from the audience. Jonny said to himself: *the old gags never fail.* Holding a few prompt cards in his slinged hand he seamlessly and eloquently guided the audience through his and Richard's relationship, their aquatic history and their short racing career.

He spoke of their first meeting at The Cellars. He briefed them on the inaugural regatta and effortlessly rolled their story through to the present. As was his style, it was interspersed with one-liners and a joke or two. Of course, he could but spill the beans on Richard's various indiscretions afloat, and ashore, during the week just past – but ever the professional, he avoided anything personal concerning Richard and Samantha's developing love story or indeed Wednesday's spat with brother Chisholme, tempting though it was.

However, Richard was not going to escape from this public speaking business so easily. Jonny – now in full flow – turned, checked that Richard was still on his feet, and delivered a no-escape ultimatum. Poor old Richard was caught flat-footed.

'At this point, ladies and gentlemen, I'm sure you would like to know the real story behind our bruised and battered bodies …?' The competitors, one and all, responded expectant with loud applause.

'Fellow crews, I now invite my skipper to explain.' More applause. Richard stared at him – he couldn't believe that Jonny would have pulled such a stunt. Before he knew what was happening Samantha, intrigued, had released her grip. She gently palmed her boy forwards, towards the 'pit'.

The audience roared their encouragement. Those infamous butterflies had grown into bats. Richard was experiencing a spasm of pressure the like of which he had not felt since his 11 Plus exam – which he subsequently failed. However, Jonny – casually – rescued the situation by launching into a question and answer session.

'Now then skipper,' he said, removing the microphone from its stand. He was now playing to all the fellow crews in the audience. 'What's your view on the current 'cruelty to crews' debate?'

Richard squirmed. Jonny went on to cite, incident by incident, their relationship balance. Richard, of course, took it all in good heart, and by the end of the session he was giving as good as he was getting.

'In conclusion, Mr Commodore,' Jonny said, winding up the session, 'and on behalf of the competitors' – he turned to the audience – 'may I offer to you, your officers and the many volunteers our sincere thanks and congratulations for a fabulously memorable week in Torbay both on, and off, the water.'

Before he could replace the microphone, and to everyone's surprise, Richard seized it from Jonny's hand!

'Ummm – can you hear me back there? In echoing my crew's comments, I would like to take this opportunity,' – the crowd was silent and he placed his hand on Jonny's shoulder – 'to thank this guy, Jonny Dubois, personally from the bottom of my heart.'

He paused again – for much longer than before. Samantha was edgy, she looked on nervously, Penny was standing, both hands pressing on her cheeks; all were thinking, where is this going? Will he, can he, continue? Jonny just stood there, in statue mode his eyes focused, on the floor...

'I thank him for his patience and undying support over these past years,' (he was swallowing hard, the bottom lip was going) 'because the reality is that without you, mate, this achievement would have remained just another of my shadow chasing fantasies.' Waiting for the wave of applause to die down he raised the microphone closer to his mouth, taking a deep breath, while Jonny hugged him. Richard said:

'Come on everyone. Three cheers for our hosts!' The tent responded with aplomb ... Hip, hip... hooray! Replacing the microphone, he turned, looked Jonny straight in the face.

'Wipe your eyes and close that mouth big boy,' he said. 'There's too much air getting in.' Richard had finally, finally, got the last word on Jonny. As the stage-party dismounted and before Richard could even speak to Samantha, Roland grabbed both him and his daughter by their arms.

'I think this deserves a small family celebration. Now, where's our Henry?'

If Richard had any plans to whisk Samantha away for private romantic merriment, they had been well and truly trumped. Swamped by both Roland's generosity and the steady stream of well-wishers to the commodore's table that evening, the remainder of Richard's night was a whirlwind. Before anyone realised, the national anthem was playing, signalling the end of festivities.

'Is it that time already?' Richard mouthed to his lady. They were now finally beside each other, her head nestling on his left shoulder.

He was at peace with the world.

'On your feet, everyone,' the commodore instructed – and that was that.

Well, it wasn't actually. At Roland's behest their party transferred back to the Chisholme residence where both Richard and Jonny were introduced to the delights of dark navy rum.

Among other brands, bottles of Pussars, Lambs and Mount Gay were produced from an amply stocked drinks cabinet. And so, ably supported by son Henry, Roland commenced his master class. Samantha and Penny retired to their respective sleeping quarters around 2:30 a.m., while the boys continued their kamikaze celebrations into the dawn...

Chapter Twenty

The Morning After...

Predictably it was to be a female only breakfast that Saturday morning. But at the stroke of nine old father Roland appeared. Fully dressed, complete with cravat, and in appearance at least, he seemed none the worse for wear.

'Morning ladies, sleep well?' he said, but with an apologetic undertone. 'Hope we didn't make too much noise.' Penny was all too aware of the noise. Jonny had missed the bed and bounced off the side table. Regardless of her broken sleep pattern she was nevertheless dressed for the journey home: cut-off denims and red t-shirt, make-up applied. Samantha looked casual by comparison: turquoise shell suit, pink toenails, no make-up.

Roland had wandered over to the window. He was whistling to himself. No recognisable tune, just a whistle.

Penny, sneaking a glance in his direction, said quietly to Samantha, 'How does he do it?' Samantha smiled, turned up the volume on the transistor. Otis Reading's version of 'Satisfaction'. It had a dual effect: it drowned out Roland and offered an opportunity for a quick bare-foot bop.

'Think he might just be little delicate on the inside, but we'll soon see. Hey, Daddy, some bacon and eggs?'

'Yes my dear, just the ticket – any porridge on the go?' The girls had their answer. Samantha, after a few forays to the cooker, realised that she wasn't feeling one hundred per cent herself. Her empathetic side couldn't help wondering just what sort of state her family had got her beloved into. By ten Jonny had joined the breakfast party. But unlike Roland, food was the last thing on his mind – by 10:15 he was making for the door…

'Still no movement from Richard or Henry?' Samantha called after him, but to no avail.

'Right then,' she said. She had decided to move things along. 'I'm going wake those two faders. Your dawn revelling is all very well Daddy but we've all got things to do today.'

Her father was, or seemed to be, oblivious. The radio was now blasting out 'It's a Man's World'. Penny turned the volume down. Glancing across at Roland, and with a large helping of sarcasm said: 'How true.'

He concerned himself with the contents of his breakfast platter. The salvo was lost in an overture of crunching toast. Jonny had returned to the kitchen. His pallor remained, with more than a hint of eau de nil. He was quiet. He was in dire need of a little sympathy. He reported briefly on activities above stairs...

'Some movement from Rich. I passed him on the landing – not looking too clever, your boy.' That was Jonny's sole contribution to the proceedings. Penny finally succumbed to his pining; a kiss and a hug seemed to lift his mood. Across the open-plan kitchen Samantha had armed herself with some lightly buttered toast and a strong brown tea in a West Ham mug – Henry's. She glanced apprehensively through the door, towards the stairs, expecting first sight at any moment of a surely heavily hung over Richard. The best Jonny could manage was a glass of water. Penny had continued to arrange their final packing. She complimented herself on her foresight: transferring the Volvo from the campsite to the Chisholme driveway before heading down to the marquee had been a wise move. With no further visible support for her ailing boy, she was determined to be on the road north by 12:00 noon. She would be doing the driving...

Richard, on returning from the bathroom, had re-deposited himself face-down on the bed. Samantha set her breakfast offering on the bedside table. She leant over to present her boy with a good morning kiss...

'Oh my God Richard, you reek of rum!'

'Your bloody father has a lot to answer for.'

Smirking, she administered a playful smack on his striped trunks. She crossed the room; slid open the sash window a few inches and allowed a rush of fresh Devon air into the room. She quietly hoped that it would dilute the stale stench of alcohol, infused with a cocktail of drunken farts and burps. Although this was not the image of Richard she would have wished for first thing in the morning, staff nurse Chisholme had seen worse on a Saturday night in casualty.

'You were all willing participants as far as I could see. Could be worse though? You should see the state of poor Jonny. It's going to be a long journey home for him – Penny's in her element.'

'My poor mate; oh, my poor head,'

'Stop your whingeing Ricky, and drink your tea,' she instructed, with a wry smile. 'I expect you up, washed and shaved and downstairs in half an hour.'

At that she bent over him, clasped his head in her warm hands and planted a kiss on his rum-caked lips. For him, it was like a flat battery being jump started..!

Smiling broadly now, Samantha left, closing the door carefully behind her. Before going down the stairs she childishly banged a couple of times on Henry's door. She rejoined the kitchen group, wistfully relaying the scene she had just encountered.

It was well after noon on a beautiful, still Devon Saturday. The champions' party had assembled on the gravel driveway to wave Penny and a now slightly more colourful Jonny on their way. Henry even emerged for the sending off, albeit from behind the curtain of his bedroom window.

In what had obviously been a well-planned pre-prize giving operation, Richard had had deposited a complete change of clothes and toiletries at the Chisholme residence. Dressed for the day, he and the now coutured Samantha strolled off hand-in-hand to the camp site. Their first duty was to perform the final hand over of the beloved *Satisfaction.* Richard's twinge of sadness soon evaporated under the weight of the Wilsons' cheque.

The striking of the awning and tents followed. Jim's VW was at last fully loaded for its return journey on Monday. And Richard, he too was finally organised, albeit because Samantha did most of the work. Bending over had become quite perilous for him; not particularly because of queasiness – more, he realised, to do with the fact he was still a bit pissed.

They brought the van back to the Chisholme's and transferred to the Beetle. To the haunting sounds of the Zombies, they slipped away to enjoy the delights of the local countryside, and hopefully a late pub lunch. Richard was now starving, and suffering from both indigestion and the effects of a serious drooth.

As Samantha navigated the back lanes of the county he confided that he would never touch dark rum again for the rest of his drinking life. And with that, he politely requested that she pull over for a moment… Samantha Chisholme was sort of enjoying her new boy's demise.

Having learnt from Penny the full reason for Richard's dramatic reaction to events at the prize giving, she was very much in a mischievous mood that fine August day. She remained at a loss, however, to understand how someone so meticulous in their everyday work, with such a compulsion for research and planning, could have failed not only to unravel her family connections, especially after the 'incident', and had remained unaware, that she was the commodore's daughter.

'I mean', she said, 'everyone knew that.'

'Sorry, what did you say pet?' asked Richard, coming to terms with his bursting head.

'Nothing Dearest, just thinking aloud', replied Samantha, suddenly a little flushed.

'Thinking? Thinking about what, pet?'

Poor Richard, he'd walked straight into her web... Instigated by Jonny – in revenge for the interrogations he had frequently suffered at the hands of his love-struck mate in recent times – tailored by Penny but importantly, approved by herself, she planned to put Richard through the wringer.

Her plan had been to allow him the enjoyment of lunch at a place in Totnes. Then, at an opportune moment, probably over coffee or a pint, to commence *her* interrogations. But with such an obvious opportunity presented on a plate, nay, on a silver salver!

'So, Ricky; tell me…'

Chapter Twenty-one

Parting of the Ways

Monday came all too soon. It was 6 a.m. as Samantha glided silently into Richard's room. Slipping under his sheets she presented him with a sumptuous good morning embrace. This is the best alarm call *I've* ever experienced, he quietly admitted. He returned the favour. They lay embraced for several minutes.

By seven it was time for the worst part of his adventure in Devon – the parting of the ways. With tears streaming, it was their final embrace. Then with a parting kiss the VW crunched out of the Chisholme driveway, Richard headed northwards, and home.

Samantha spent the remainder of the day in her bedroom. After some gentle persuasion she finally emerged for afternoon tea, eyes red and puffy.

Her father hugged her and said, 'He's the one then.'

No reply was needed, just a squeeze of hands.

Chapter Twenty-two

The Office

Richard had had the foresight to book Monday off. The factory was more or less directly on the home run. Predictably, he decided to call by his office. If nothing else, he had convinced himself that it would be wise to discover what tomorrow's arrangements were for his newly elevated status. Nothing at all to do with the big silver cup which lay nestled within a sports bag on the front seat of the VW – no, Richard wasn't that vain…

His colleagues, of course, knew him only too well. They were expecting him. Their lunch break had been spent decorating, but they worried that he would be early; Fred, the factory gateman, had been pre-warned. They weren't wrong.

A shred of disappointment washed over Richard as he awaited clearance from the dithering Fred. The VW's registration didn't match Richard's usual car number. 'Ah for pity's sake Fred...' He had by now created a personalised local hero status, but could see no visible signs to celebrate his accomplishment. *The least they could have done was pin up a well done banner for me.*

'Oh well, me and my expectations,' he said as he closed the van door. With shoulders dropped and hands in pockets he walked across the tarmac and around the flower bed to the front door. The reception area brought him up short. He stood and stared. There were banners, bunting and balloons a-plenty. The entire office was down there, including his supervisor Jim, senior purchasing manager Joe, and to cap it off, the company's managing director!

A wave of emotion washed over him. He had been expectant, prepared but faced with the reality, he paled and clammed up.

A colleague was quietly despatched to the VW to retrieve the champion's cup. Charles Whitworth, the MD, kicked off proceedings with a few well-chosen words. He included mention of his personal visit to the venue; he claimed to have spoken to Richard and smilingly informed the gathering that Richard had absolutely no idea who he was: 'Far too busy signing autographs.'

Richard did muster a response. It was by no means in Jonny's league but with the cup now on display and inspected in some detail by the various sporting aficionados within the company, it diverted attention from him. The formalities were completed with much back-slapping and hand-shaking. With equal gusto came a steady stream of comments on Richard's fine black eye, and it was almost an hour before the session wound up.. Without further ado, it was the time to depart.

Joe Martin walked Richard back to the van and said his personal congratulations while commenting that the MD, 'old Whitey', was most impressed.

'He didn't come up here specially?' Richard enquired naively.

'No, no, there were board meetings on here today. But I'll tell you son, he did comment on how well you handled yourself down there. The way you dealt with the obvious pressure of competition. He confided that he was looking forward to chatting to you when all the fuss dies down.'

Joe's impression was that he wanted to pick the champ's brains, his boat brain.

'It'll give him a bit of one-upmanship in the yacht club, and of course the board room too, if you see what I mean.'

Richard felt a tingle running down his spine.

'Flippin 'eck Joe, you never know who you're talking to – hope I didn't ignore him.'

Richard remained a little flustered: it wasn't so much the surprise of the reception – he was sort of prepared for that – it was the intensity of it all. A week ago he was little Richard the junior buyer, but today…

Joe just smiled. 'Richard,' he said, 'report to my office in the morning. Okay son?'

'Yes boss will do, and many, many thanks for today.' They shook on it, and as he turned away Joe replied:

'Pleasure, you deserved it. Have a good night's sleep – big day tomorrow.'

The engine was fired up, and Richard was on the final leg of the return journey. Next stop: the presentation of his champions cup to the family, the whole circle. This would hopefully include his now-favourite uncle. The cup would of course have pride of place in his mum's trophy cabinet.

Chapter Twenty-three

Fatality and a Brace of Opportunities

Joe Martin, a tall, gangly man in his late fifties, was in his day a fierce and – in spite of his frame – successful competitor in the Midlands motorcycle scrambling scene. He was well aware that Richard's attention would often be wandering back to Torbay, a fact around which he had sympathetically devised his new work schedule.

Fashion follower Richard presented himself that morning in a restrained charcoal-grey crimplene suit. A pale blue high-collared bri-nylon shirt was fronted with a red-flowered kipper tie. Not unexpectedly, he was in early. It was just after 7a.m. That was well before Joe. Joe appeared some time after eight. As was the norm, Joe's day commenced with a black coffee. That was Richard's first task. By ten o'clock the new job had been outlined in loose terms. Richard was somewhat taken aback by the apparent scale of his promotion.

He had reasoned that his general responsibilities would of course be broadened, but in manageable increments. He had fully expected to be eased into his new role. He reasoned that promotion would see him handling a more valuable range of products. There would be introductions to the principal suppliers; key product ranges would follow; his purchasing portfolio would expand as his competence level allowed. This was, after all, a very conservative family firm.

Joe Martin's news that the department had been restructured had caught him off-guard. Perhaps he had been too focused on sailing matters to have tapped into the office gossip. Not only was he to share a brand new office with Jim Jones, whom last week he looked up to as his supervisor, but from here on they would be sitting as equals, side by side, sharing responsibilities. Momentarily this brought back the infamous butterflies. Generally, however, Richard remained, outwardly at least, unfazed by the prospect. He was apprehensive though, but he reasoned, with great maturity, that if he could win a national title against the odds, he could do this.

Joe, Jim and Richard had convened a formal meeting in the new office at 12:00 noon. This was to agree the integration details of the restructure. Blinds were down. The outside open office purred with concern; rumour and speculation were rampant. There formed a 'friendship queue' where everyone, it seemed, had become Richard's bosom buddy.

Joe opened proceedings. 'Jim here will continue to manage the buying of base raw materials for the factory. You, Richard, overseeing a new team of three, will take on overall procurement, and the management of what we term accessories. 'Accessories', Richard soon realised, covered a huge mandate and ranged from consumables to factory spares, accounting for a mammoth site outlay.

Yes, it was an unwieldy and complicated brief. Outwardly Richard had presented a facade as cool as Jonny behind the microphone, but even inside he was actually fairly calm. He had served his time under Jim, and Jim knew the ropes. The only difference, he concluded, was the size of the new operation. Having personally brought several untidy portfolios under control previously, this brief therefore posed no major issues; after all, he now had the luxury of three assistants.

Richard's enthusiasm, verging on cockiness, was somewhat tempered when Joe added a caveat:

'The board' he said, 'want this [£] outlay reduced by fifteen percent immediately. And by a further ten percent over the forthcoming six months. 'No wonder everyone is being nice to me, Richard thought, suddenly crestfallen.

There was more...

'The number of suppliers to the site needs culled by thirty per cent, and by year-end!'

Joe looked Richard straight in the eye: 'We can do it, son.'

Jim nodded in support, but Richard wasn't so sure that he was fully onside. 'Let's get you introduced to your A Team,' said Jim.

The meeting ended at 14:20 hours.

Richard returned to his desk – *his* desk. Then, some ten minutes later, he and Jim were alone. Jim took the opportunity to open up to Richard, now somewhat overwhelmed, not to say starving – it had been a long time since his early breakfast.

'Lad, I'm coming 63, and I want to ease myself into the background. I've been doing this job for too many years. Now that things are picking up again I need to back off a bit. So, this was deemed to be the perfect time to reorganise for the future.' With some purpose, he got up from his somewhat dilapidated self-sculpted chair, closed the door and widened his 'sermon'. The blinds remained down; there was privacy. It was needed.

'Richard...' he continued, 'you may not realise it lad, but *you* are now seen as the blue-eyed boy round here. This is your opportunity to shine. Maybe even get yourself promoted further in time. Get a move down to head office and the bright lights of Bristol.'

'Yeah sure – but why me?' replied a now somewhat sceptical Richard.

'Your buying skills are well documented; I took some credit for that. But it's that competitive spirit. I know that you had no idea about all this.' He paused. Richard was all ears, a little embarrassed if he was honest. 'Let's just say a close interest was taken down there; not so much for any victory, but in how you handled yourself under pressure. Why do you think old Whitworth would take the trouble to just *drop in*?' Jim was in his stride now. 'Okay, I know he does a bit of boating and all that yachty stuff, but lad, he lives miles away from Torquay. Rich, there are big expansion plans afoot. I am very much of the opinion that your success in Devon convinced not only Whitworth but Joe and some of the other directors, that there is a lot more in store for master D'Arcy!'

Richard just looked at him, glassy eyed.

'Now; you of course know, at least I hope you do, that I'll help you with this in every way I can, but at the end of the day the ball is, as they say, in your court lad.'

Richard had remained glued to his seat for what seemed like an eternity. Then he tried to dredge up some level-headed and businesslike remarks –with only limited success.

'Er, yeah, thanks Jim, I hear what you're saying, I think. I won't let you down.'

'Don't you worry about me lad. This is all about you and the future of this department, maybe even the site.' Jim's tone was verging on the sanctimonious now. 'The decisions that you will take – you'll have to take – won't be easy or popular. Those folks out there who last week were your friends will from tomorrow – today – be merely colleagues. Remember that: not friends, colleagues. This little fact will help when you are writing up your business plan. I'm sorry if it puts a dampener on your celebrations. Richard lad, you've heard me say it before. There is no room for sentiment in business, or buying!'

'Business plan?' The two words struck terror.

'Don't worry lad, we'll do it together; make sure your pencils are sharp tomorrow.' Jim attempted to re-settle his new partner. 'Tell you what lad, why don't you take yourself offside. Get some air. When you come back at, say, half three, we'll make a start then. Okay?'

'Yeah. Fab, Jim. I'll nip across the road for a chip. Be back on a full stomach, rarin to go.'

As Jim opened his lunch box another salad peered out at him.

'That health food; it'll be the death of you Jim.'

Richard stopped at reception on his way out. He nipped into a side room where frequently he would interview cold-calling commercial travellers. A two tone Trimfone sat alone on faux mahogany table. In the relative privacy of a bare wood panelled room he dialled 9 for an outside line. When the tone changed his forefinger dialled Samantha's number. He just had to tell her his earth-shattering, life-changing news.

Roland answered, said she was at the hospital. He tried Jonny – he was also out. Finally, he caught up with his dad, who heard him out offered his congratulations and wisely advised his boy to listen well, and take proper notes. Arthur's reaction to Richard's news had telegraphed a loud emotion of fatherly pride. However, both knew that a celebration would be put on ice. He would have a busy evening digesting and planning, if he lasted that long…

Life at the office remained manic for the remainder of the year. Sharing a plush office didn't turn out to be the palatial experience that Richard had expected. Big Jim, at twenty-something stone, was a sixty-a-day man: this was combined with a terrible diet. His salad days – obviously a belated effort to lose weight – had been long since consigned to various bins. All that, plus some personal hygiene issues, made their 'living quarters' somewhat reminiscent of the old sailing club's changing room on warm, wet day.

However, Jim was a patient and considerate teacher. Richard, in turn, had been learning fast. He needed to, because on one bleak December morning he was unexpectedly summoned to Joe Martin's office.

No jaunty good mornings on this occasion. Joe closed the door immediately; placed his right hand on Richard's shoulder.

'I've some bad news for you boy.'

Richard's pallor suddenly drained – he hadn't much natural colour to start with. Instinct told him not to listen to the next line. His immediate fear was that his bubble was about to be burst. Joe was not his normal easy self. He couldn't look Richard in the eye.

He was fidgety and very tense. Finally he spoke, but quietly, hesitantly; almost in a whisper.

'Richard, what— what I have to tell—tell you, is not easy—' Richard's stomach churned audibly. After another pause, eyes blinking, darting around the room, Joe continued:

'Jim Jones. Jim was found dead in the early hours of this morning; sounds as if he may have suffered a massive heart attack or maybe it was a stroke...'

This was not the news that Richard thought Joe was about to deliver. Other than the passing of his granny a few years ago, Richard had never experienced death before – certainly not sudden death. He found himself in no man's land. He tried to disguise the fact that he felt relief as well as grief. Whether it was the thought of demotion or even losing his job, or indeed the realisation that Jim would no longer be by his side, the shock had kicked in. He was knocked off-balance, grateful for the back of the leather upholstered chair into which his fingers were biting.

Joe and Jim went back a long way. Richard could easily see that his senior manager was in some distress. In his natural gangly stance he looked fragile. Richard took his arm and gently directed him to his chair. He offered condolences. Taking control of the developing situation, Richard seemed to find a maturity which belied his youth. Joe seated, slouched against his desk he clutched his faithful coffee mug with both hands, it was empty. There was no more conversation. Richard melted away; he would await instructions.

After some rearranging of three diaries, Richard drove Joe, in Joe's Rover, to Jim's home; a compact pebble dashed bungalow, varnished front door. This Jim had shared with an aging sister, Jessie. Richard stopped short of entering, allowing Joe the space to be a part of the family's private grief. He stretched out and found himself – not without some guilt – enjoying the plush tan interior of this company car. Retuning the radio to Radio One he dreamed that maybe someday...

Following the Christmas holidays and towards the end of January, Richard's journey was to step up another gear. Jim's position not being replaced, he was presented with the prospect of becoming the sole buyer for the factory. With the addition of Joe's not wholly unexpected announcement that he would retire at the end of the year, this provided the champion with a brace of opportunities. They were loud and clear – if he decided to take on the challenge.

Jonny's prospects too were moving apace. Having graduated with first class honours he was offered, among others, a position with a leading dental practice in Edinburgh. This he accepted. Jonny had quickly become resident in the northern capital; a rented one-bed flat in Musselburgh to the east, overlooking the Firth of Forth, became his base. It was basic in the extreme but offered a commute of a mere twenty-five minutes, by bus. Later he took up an option on a two-up, two-down terraced house in Penicuik. It was further out but the house was superior and the area more upmarket. But the clincher was that Penny had by then also graduated; she too had soon moved north of the border, joining him in Penicuik. A targeted position within the Edinburgh arts scene provided her with a career start.

It wasn't long before their living regime began to take on an air of permanence. Penicuik turned out to be a short-term arrangement, its sale realising an impressive profit. They didn't move too far, and their next property boasted two reception rooms, three bedrooms, and toilets upstairs and down...

Meanwhile, Richard found himself managing a galloping work schedule in tandem with the development of a long-distance romance. Samantha remained in Devon. That was home for her. On the sporting front, a whole new level of challenges was to emerge, but meantime location issues, lengthy train journeys and career fast-tracking somehow had to be accommodated. With Jonny resident in Edinburgh; Richard anywhere between the north of England, the south coast and, with increasing frequency, Belfast, Milan and Stockholm, their new sailing season needed cruel planning, not to say pruning.

Their title defence in August was ring-fenced. The trip to Ireland booked. All other circuit regattas had to be examined before any semblance of a campaign could be agreed. It took most of one weekend to agree – the perfect excuse for a get-together. It was Richard and Samantha's first visit to Edinburgh, and indeed Scotland. She drove up to Birmingham, met up with Richard and from there they flew up to the Scottish capital. It was a bitterly cold February weekend, but the four of them managed the full tour, packed in a good deal of socialising and more or less sorted the programme for the incoming season.

Chapter Twenty-four

Long-distance Relationships

After Torbay, Richard and Samantha's championship romance was undeniably under some pressure. Yes, there were the obligatory daily telephone conversations and a steady stream of two-way love letters. But hospital shift work and Richard's immediate workload were physically keeping the couple apart. In fact it was to be several weeks before they were able align diaries. It seemed like an eternity before Richard and Samantha finally met up, and indeed consummated, their relationship.

After some sisterly persuasion, Hilary Chisholme 'voluntarily' gave up his Bristol house to allow that reunion to take place. There had been devious goings-on behind the scenes. Samantha and her brother's long-term partner, Adrianne, hatched a plot to lure Hilary down to London for *their* weekend reunion: for a month or so Adrianne had been home spending time with her aging parents in central France.

This venue, Hilary's house, was a compromise, a sort of halfway house, albeit still constituting a serious round trip for Richard. But love and a lust-fuelled heart knows nothing of excessive mileage. And with new wheels under him, he was a more than willing participant.

Uncle Jim had come up trumps again. This time he had sourced a Triumph Stag for his nephew to trial. Okay, it wasn't yellow, but in white it still cut quite a dash. The deal was that Richard could take it for the weekend; in the following week, he and its owner could perhaps agree a deal. However, Richard made no-one aware, during negotiations, that there was something of a 200-mile round trip involved in the trial. He was a professional buyer after all...

Having got away early on the Friday afternoon, Samantha was surprised – elated– to see him arrive by mid-evening. Their bodies merged. The cherry-painted front door slammed. A bursting dam of passion was released.

They remained submerged for the remainder of the night, surfacing at intervals for air, their reunion passionate, enthusiastic, still, loud, quiet, physical, tender... They had no time to waste – certainly no time to enjoy the delights of this fine period dwelling and its rich and tasteful decor. Big brother Hilary was due to return from his own liaisons on the Sunday evening to reclaim occupation.

Whilst Samantha obviously held the key to Hilary's cold and unrelenting personality, there remained no connection between him and Richard. In fact their little contretemps had never been spoken of since – certainly he wasn't going to dredge it up again.

It was the dawn chorus that roused Richard. Slanting through venetian blinds, the early morning September sun cast slits of light onto the contours of their entwined nakedness. With Samantha nestling, spooned in his arms, he delicately explored the perfection her tanned body offered. There he remained, captivated, glued by her warm softness.

08:30 hours: the Sony Digimatic radio alarm broke the silence. It was droning out Leonard Cohen's *'Susanna'*. Samantha awoke slowly. Morning kisses glided them into another embrace. As she continued to drift, Richard's predatory instincts were aroused. Realising that he was starving, he silently exited the bedroom. He stole a final glance at her whilst grabbing a gown off the door peg. To bound naked through someone else's house would, he figured, be uncool. Modestly, he navigated the trail of discarded clothing down the stairs, towards the kitchen, and breakfast.

Arriving at his destination he realised that this was perhaps not Hilary's personal gown. A bit skimpy but at least it covered his modesty. *'Wouldn't do if the neighbours got a bit over-excited.'* But then he realised that he stood out, nay, radiated, in glaring purple with a contrasting lime-green Japanese embroidered embellishment.

He still wondered. Na, it couldn't. It couldn't be his; definitely too short.

Realising suddenly that he had actually been modelling it, Richard suffered an unusual bout of self-consciousness – even though he clearly had the legs to carry it. Looking around, he glanced through the kitchen window, checking for admirers. He corpsed. Sniggering became full-on laughter. Finally, with arms outstretched, he proclaimed aloud:

'I think purple really does suit me..!'

A love bird's breakfast in bed was delivered – when Richard appeared, resplendent as a rainbow, it was Samantha's turn to have convulsions. After breakfast they bathed, and finally they were dressed. An exploration of the house's mature gardens front and rear followed. They soon retired indoors, persistent drizzle having replaced the morning sun.

They talked, cuddled, laughed, talked more and continued to unlock the secret slices of their past lives, while sharing ambitions and dreams. Richard was, of course, totally bemused to discover that his preening, his early courtship moves, were in general a complete waste of energy. He had already been 'selected' prior to that unforgettable upmarket training day.

In fact he had never realised that Samantha was one of the trio of girls he had unsuccessfully plied with bribery cocktails on the Saturday evening of his inaugural regatta.

'Actually,' Samantha teased, 'It was Jonny who caught my eye, but as he was already claimed, I settled for you.'

'Oh bloody typical, second best again.'

'Poor Richard, you really had no idea.' She softly stroked his cheek, then gave him a stern look. 'But, Ricky my boy, you were very close to blowing yourself completely out of the water at our next encounter, remember?'

'Yeah, yeah I know; can't we just forget that indiscretion? After all I'm just a rough northern lad at heart. And, in all honestly you did – I mean you do – have great legs and a...' Richard paused, realising that with every word he was digging an even deeper hole. Then he continued, 'See? Look what you're doing to me – I'm all over the place again...'

'Well okay, but remember this: life's far too short to forgive and forget!' Richard just looked at her for a moment, not knowing whether this was another of her wind-ups. She laughed. Richard leant over and kissed her again, and again.

'So,' he said finally, 'who was that girl who actually blew me out that evening? I know it wasn't you. I mean I'd obviously remember you. And another thing, something that's been puzzling me ...' He hesitated. 'You live down south, as far south as can be. What on earth brought you all the way north, twice?'

'So many questions, Ricky.' Samantha fell back into the softness of the sofa. 'Let's see. Long black hair, heavily made up eyes? That

is, or rather was, Alice Forsythe; she's married again, just recently –
bit of a man eater. She would have devoured you Ricky my boy...'

Richard bit his lip and said nothing for a moment. Then he
replied:

'Na, not me – don't think so.'

He was still more than a little intrigued by her globe-trotting.

'Come on then. Why were you up north? Spying for the southern
parliament or something...?'

'Actually,' she said, 'I go up there fairly regularly – I have
girlfriends you know. That's why I was up at *that* event. We
actually lived around Chester; I grew up there. I was in my teens
when we moved down south. First it was Cheltenham, then a few
years later, onto Devon. But I've kept up with good friends. It's our
little gang: old school friends, the five of us. Yep, we've stayed
close, all these years – girls do that kind of thing'.

'And the sailing?'

'Well yes, I suppose that was a bit odd. Our PE class sort of split
itself between swimming, netball and hockey. Then an opportunity
to try out boating appeared. To be truthful Ricky, it wasn't the
attraction of the sailing; no, our gang… well, we were more
interested in the boys at the sailing club.' Richard hung on every
word. 'In the end,' she continued, 'only Alice, Georgia and me, took
to it, but we've all remained close friends.' She sighed. 'As
frequently as time and money allow, we organise visits. Georgia,

she's married too, lives outside Norwich now. She's not boating anymore; a shame 'cos, she was really good.'

'And?' Richard hurried her along. 'Your day at the posh training course? Remember that day? The day you damned near got me crippled for life?'

'Poor Ricky. You never suspected a thing, did you babe?' She smiled teasingly. 'It was actually Alice who hatched to the plot.' Samantha's lips widened into a wicked grin – she enjoyed being mischievous. 'She was hooked up with one of the guys from that club at the time. He had signed up for the training.' She was now looking directly at Richard. 'But the week before, she broke her wrist. We had some fun teasing her about the circumstances…'

'Get on with it,' said Richard.

'... and rather than letting him down, Alice – remember Alice?' He nodded. 'She persuaded me to stand in as substitute crew. That was with Vincent. Vincent with the huge hair, remember?'Richard nodded again – hadn't a clue who she was referring to.

'I wasn't that keen at first, I mean it was a 500 mile round trip and a long train ride. But when she mentioned that you and Jonny had also signed up I decided there and then – shouldn't be telling you this – to go boy chasing!'

After a pause and a sip of white wine she continued. 'The folks paid the train and bus fares. And as well as re-connecting with you' – she leant across and kissed him – 'we, the girls, had a lovely long weekend together; Friday afternoon to Monday morning.'

Samantha leant back, arms folded. 'So, Ricky my boy, you can imagine my great disappointment when you first opened your big northern mouth. Just as well I can see past first impressions, eh?'

She thumped Richard on the shoulder, knocking him into the corner pit of the Parker Knoll, following through and diving on top of him. There followed an unexpected pause in the conversation.

After repositioning herself somewhat formally at the other end of the sofa, protected by a wall of comfort cushions, she picked up the glass again and continued to unlock her past. She and Richard had realised that with one thing and another, this weekend was the first opportunity they'd had to truthfully and soulfully talk. With the restrictions of first time sex beautifully concurred talking was easy and honest.

Now twenty two – Richard was four years her elder – she had enjoyed a pretty eventful life. Samantha was a surprise parcel for Roland and her mother Edith; premature at five pounds and seven ounces. Henry had entered the world seven years before her, and Hilary was the eldest at thirty-three. Always a clever and adventurous child, she breezed through school and on to university, hardly pausing for breath. The apple of her father's eye, she was hopelessly spoiled by her parents. Her brothers, however, would often redress the balance in the rough and tumble of everyday growing up.

This was especially true, she recalled, when it came to negotiating her early teenage years. Both brothers would regularly monitor and question her choice of companion. Hilary could be particularly protective of his little sister. It seemed, she confided to Richard, that many a would-be suitor found himself bloodied and stunned in a hedge near their house.

Some things, Richard thought (but didn't dare say), never seem to change. He smiled awkwardly.

She described how the family had moved to Paignton some years later, and how the biggest shock in her early life was probably when she dropped out of university. Richard hung on her every word. She said she had determined to follow father and Henry into architecture. There was no question but that this would be her calling. The family honour was to be upheld. Alas, a year in she realised that it was not for her. She felt awful for her father, and her misery was compounded by homesickness, and the end of a long-term romance that had started in school.

With semi-glazed eyes, she explained how she persevered with the course, unwilling to let her father down. How she arrived home one Easter, gaunt and listless, weighing in at some seven stone. She would never forget the look on her mother's face when she saw the transformation: shock and concern in equal measures.

Without rushing, she quietly explained to a captivated Richard that eventually that chapter of depression had ended. With strong support from her parents, especially her father, her life – a new life really – had meaning again, the crash site cleared, as it were, of emotional debris. Doors reopened and paths were smoothed, allowing her to revisit the catalogue of career choices.

It was perhaps no coincidence that medicine figured large among her options. From her teen years she had discovered in herself a caring and compassionate nature. Frequently and with relish she would accompany her mother, then a district nurse, on her community rounds to tend the sick, the elderly and the needy.

'I loved those times, being out with Mum. God, I really miss her.' Samantha paused, used another tissue. 'It turned out that Mum had doubted whether architecture was the right course, and was a little disappointed at my unwillingness to consider other options. I must have been a right snotty brat.'

After a long summer of recuperation, a revitalised Samantha Chisholme entered the health service. She never looked back. Her mother was delighted.

Richard, enthralled but unsure what to say, made an attempt to lighten the atmosphere by quizzing her on that school romance. She gave nothing away. The only titbit she offered was that she had recently seen the guy pushing a buggy around town. Probing further, Richard was firmly cut off. He had not fully realised how completely Samantha had opened up her heart to him.

'Previous romances and relationships are not up for discussion!' she said. 'Babe, I won't probe into your past encounters, or should I say conquests, so the same applies to mine – not that I had many.' With that Samantha clammed. She rose abruptly. Another tell-tale tear seeped. With some haste, she made for the kitchen, obviously a little upset. She uttered one word in an exasperated tone. Richard didn't pick it up but nevertheless, he gasped.

Oh my God, I've done it again! Why can't I keep my big mouth shut? You always cross that line. Richard was full of remorse. But he didn't dither. He immediately followed, to make peace. Samantha was returning with the same intention, and they met halfway. One thing led to another and in due course they found themselves back in the bedroom for, as Richard commented later, a session on conflict resolution.

Their weekend, whilst frustratingly brief, was delightfully perfect. Richard, now obviously to be known as 'Ricky', determined that it should remain so and grow stronger. He was prepared no matter what to avoid any further conflict.

Painful though it would be, he must be gone before Hilary's tyres crunched on the gravel driveway. Out of sight, out of mind: he figured that this was the best option in the circumstances. Whilst he was certainly not known for backing off or running away from confrontation, on this occasion he was not prepared to allow anything to break the spell of their romantic fantasia.

After a light evening meal it was back to the all-too-familiar goodbyes and tear-soaked kisses. By 7:30 p.m. in the fallen darkness of a spent Bristol evening, the Stag's beguilingly gurgly exhaust accompanied him in pursuit of the M6 north. The long drive home gave Richard a chance to get some clear thought into, and the garbage out of, his love-struck head. He finally decided that it would be he who would take the first step in bridging the gulf with Sam's brother. He was now content that his decision to leave when he did was the correct one. Confrontation, if any, could wait.

Samantha too, now alone, was trying to keep her emotions in check. Hilary's house had reverted to pristine: bed changed, washing done. She was generally keeping busy, awaiting her brother's return. More important was Richard's 'I'm safely home' telephone call. He did take the number? She worried. Hilary was delayed. Her carefully prepared supper of thanksgiving was consigned to the bin. This act in itself was enough to tip the balance of her emotions. Already she was missing her boy.

Late home, Richard called to report his safe arrival and to say goodnight. Who should answer the telephone? It was a brief, polite conversation; not frosty. That next evening he penned a short letter.

Hilary, hope you're good.

...Just wanted to say thank you for opening your beautiful home to Sam and I. For me in particular it shaved huge mileage off my round trip and allowed us to spend more precious time together.

Perhaps we'll be able to meet face-to-face soon; share a pint and talk sailing?

Finally, and I realise that our first encounter could have gone better, as such I feel that I should apologise for my language on that occasion.

Kind regards, R.

He naturally assumed that Samantha would be proud of his bridge-building initiative. However, he sensed that she was perhaps not as enamoured as he thought she should be. A few weeks later, Samantha explained her lacklustre response. Knowing her brother just a little better than Richard did, she was very much of the opinion that he would take this peace offering as a sign of weakness. However, she equally didn't understand Richard's ulterior motive. The truth was, he couldn't care less whether Hilary accepted or rejected his brief peace offering. His main concern was his love for Samantha. If Hilary decided to be excluded from their relationship, well, Richard wasn't going to jump through hoops for him.

Basically, his opinion of Hilary remained on the low side. Okay, his musical taste impressed, with the exception of the three Beatles LPs he had stumbled over. Regardless of the trappings of an obviously successful operator which were displayed at the Bristol residence, Richard's mental portrait of Hilary remained unchanged: six very clever feet of pompous, arrogant, posh thug, with a personality so cold that, as even Sam had once remarked, it could inflict frostbite on a snowman. He never got a reply to the letter: he never mentioned that fact to Samantha though.

Chapter Twenty-five

1: Going Forward, Together

Three key issues challenged Richard D'Arcy. Number one was his career, followed by his sailing while number three was his emerging love life. And he must face all of them head-on. It was a three-legged stool. Ignore or break any of the legs and the whole structure would tumble. If he was ever going to strike a work/life balance he must rationalise and organise his fast-changing lifestyle. Ignoring the issues would for sure drive him into an emotional impasse. It wasn't that he couldn't see ahead, it was more that he found himself floundering in turbulent seas. But by applying his meticulous planning and growing management skills he was perfecting the art of remaining afloat. Richard was at his best when analysing a problem. Coolly he took stock, visiting each leg in turn. Slowly he was finding himself.

First, his career, his income. It was that which allowed everything else to flourish, to function. Richard D'Arcy was now enjoying the benefits, a tidy salary offered. He was also a company man, but he would never dream of admitting it to those further up the hierarchy. While his leisure life, especially his sporting exploits were driven by risk-taking Richard was never the type to gamble with employment, this was especially so, considering the climate he had just come through. The company had survived and was showing significant signs of expansion; he wanted to rise with them. So, all thing being equal, he figured that it was not a time to 'rock the boat' even though various interesting and financially attractive positions were out there. The recruitment pages bore testament to this. Richard had opted to sit tight, or at least consolidate, until his promotion potential showed its full face. However, in adopting a 'status quo' attitude, the issue of location, particularly in relation to Samantha's life, was becoming something of a conundrum. He would get to the second, and the third legs of his life planning, in due course…

2: Leg One – Bridges and Silver Linings

At work, his rise up the management ladder had not been meteoritic but it was nevertheless positive and with pace. A career path paralleled with a significantly increased work load. Together with his new departmental responsibility, he also had inherited people management, an area in which he was something of a novice.

As well as early morning starts Richard, of his own volition – and expense – had signed himself onto an evening Higher National Certificate (HNC) course in management. He ran his daily work routine autonomously, but in parallel with forfeited lunchtime periods: for example; in the study of advanced buying techniques, he would often be seen cramming, with a sandwich in one hand, pencil in the other…

Three nights a week in the not so, nearby, technical college, proved hard going. He was determined. Such was Richard's driven mindset. Success in sailing had brought him nautical fame, and romance. Succeeding in his studies, while sacrificing social life, would eventually assist, he figured, with his career aspirations – if he lasted that long.

It was no surprise when he seamlessly moved into the position of managing buyer following Joe Martin's planned retirement. His confidence and natural ability made him the obvious choice; he was the man of the moment. He had stepped onto the company's management elevator.

It provided a raft of benefits. The fully serviced company car became an invaluable asset. The Stag got parked up at Ashley Road: Arthur, complete with flat cap and driving gloves, and Molly in silk headscarf, cut a fine dash around town that summer. It came as no surprise that the new role created even more time pressures and extended travel between the factory head office in Bristol and suppliers. Richard's need for clarity and detail would often take him off-site to scrutinise prospective suppliers' claims.

An upside, however, was being able to arrange these and his southern visits to meet up with Samantha. Richard developed the fine art of so arranging business hotel accommodation that it dovetailed with his domestic arrangements. He and Samantha opportunistically expanded their available quality time. This provided a positive bridge over which their love affair strengthened. Conversely, family visits to Ashley Road were rationed, as were outings at the sailing club.

Positives vastly outweighed the negatives. He and Samantha continued to use Bristol as their hub. They spent much precious time together in and around that city. Not surprisingly, a minimum of this was shared with her brother. Richard remained stand-offish. He never felt comfortable around Hilary. With Adrianne, he was a different person.

Samantha also emerged as a strong and natural business ally. In the programme of dinners and conferences that Richard was now attending on behalf of the company, she would often be by his side when hospital shifts permitted. In her work world, the sick and infirm came first. Her priorities, she often reminded Richard, were more important than overheads measured in percentages and pounds, or dollars.

Often, in mischief, she would deliver one of her by now well-tailored pronouncements. In conversation with his colleagues or, worse, a would-be paying supplier, she would challenge the morality of capitalism in the context of the caring needs of the great unwashed. She became a natural ally though, always judging her interventions wisely. Richard's equally well-practiced response was to cup his head in his hands and declare: 'She's on her bloody soap box again.' But it was all good natured and ironically enough, Richard regularly came away with a better than expected deal.

They made a good team.

3: Leg Two – Partnerships and Engagements

Afloat, Richard's sailing activity, because of his workload and
Jonny's move to Edinburgh, had become sporadic. It had been
reduced to a programme of carefully chosen regattas. The
acquisition of Dave Gilmore's boat and a new sail wardrobe
courtesy of SSM provided them with enough edge to keep the
chasing pack at bay. Their victory margins were progressively
narrowing, but as that season wound its way through the summer the
haul of trophies continued to grow. But several of the previous
season's competitors had moved on: The twins; Smith and O'Reilly;
even John Simms. Dave Gilmore never replaced the boat, his yard
required his full attention and as for Michael, he had just
disappeared...

The 'family' outing, and much-needed holiday to see the
O'Brien's in Ireland, lived up to and indeed exceeded expectations –
and proved successful on the water.

This was the prelude to the first defence of their national title. It was August again. They both wondered where the season had gone. Bridlington was the venue. Unlike their epic encounter of last year, their defence played out as a fairly straightforward affair. Whilst they required a reasonable result in the last race of the series, their final points tally would record historically that the cup was retained with a degree of comfort. Richard did the speech!

The whole week had been easy going. It provided Richard with de-stressing downtime, away from the rigours of the workplace. Even the sudden break in the heat-wave couldn't dampen spirits. No camper vans or tents this time. Both couples enjoyed the relative luxury of the eastern seaboard's B&B tradition. Their choice of guest house however, would always bring a smile to their faces. To satisfy the moral standards of their landlady, the boys were assigned one room, the girls another. Of course, they observed the house rules...

Even before they arrived at the east coast venue, it was clear that whilst their friendship was surely to be lifelong, Richard and Jonny's sailing partnership had run its natural course. Location-wise, they were edging towards opposite ends of the country. Their respective careers were spiralling upwards. Both were harnessed with similar leisure-time constraints.

The realities, regrettable as they were, eventually had to be faced. Richard's offer to buy Jonny's share of their boat was duly accepted. Their partnership, with a tear of sadness, was officially –

and amicably – dissolved. There was consolation in a few wee drams; both of them, in their new and relative maturity, had discovered the pleasures of ; Jonny in Scotch, Richard in Irish.

'Another Glenlivet and a Black Bush please, barman, we're okay for water...'

On the following evening – a Thursday – to celebrate past times (and indeed Samantha and Richard's first anniversary) it was off to a restaurant. A re-run of the previous year's 'last supper' in Torquay it wasn't... It was more posh, and definitely pricier. However, as they waited for their table, Penny stole the show. She produced a positively luminous left finger. A white gold lattice ring adorned with small diamonds set in pairs around a central garnet, fairly lit up the company. How she contained herself Samantha would forever wonder – such a diva. What a night.

Then, later in the privacy of their B&B, as opposed to the delights of Bridlington's fisherman's quay, Richard and Samantha re-enacted the events of last year's liaison on that moonlit Torbay harbour wall, and Samantha finally offloaded her little secret – her white lie. That lie which had hauled them both back from the edge of the ultimate sexual encounter. In January 1977 Penny and Jonny married.

It was a memorable and traditional Cumbrian wedding day; Penny was a totally stunning bride, Jonny suitably regal. Jonny's older brother Keith was best man and as the eighty-six guests discovered, was equal to the groom in oratorical skill. The reception was a riot in several different ways, but Jonny's speech took the biscuit.

The happy couple honeymooned in Benidorm, and home for Mr and Mrs Dubois became the village of Queensferry, under the shadow of the Forth Bridges.

Whether it was the occasion or the romance of the big day, that night in their hotel room Richard literally took his girl's breath away. He popped *his* question. After what appeared to be a lifetime's pause, keeping him on bended knee –Samantha was good at that – she accepted. And she, thought Richard, called Penny a diva... A temporary ring was forged from a hair clip.

Later that year the Dubois' joined the Royal Forth Yacht Club, just a few miles from Queensferry. It commanded a view across the Forth estuary from the south shore at Granton Harbour in Midlothian.

After a season of sailing with various members they acquired a Dragon for themselves; it was quite elderly and needed some TLC but it was a project that Jonny and Penny threw themselves into. Archie's tutoring had obviously seeded in Jonny's mind, and both couples enjoyed weekends of sailing, and occasional competition, in Scottish waters.

4: Leg Three – Regatta Love

With Samantha at home in Torquay and Richard 'up north', diary planning was a constant preoccupation. It required picking out suitable regatta venues and weekend meeting places to coincide with Samantha's shift pattern. Their relationship, whilst no less committed, was being stretched. It was costing them a small fortune. The only constant was Richard's meeting schedule at head office in Bristol...

During the summer months it was 'regatta love' but in the off-season, and during the winter, the cold world of commerce somewhat surprisingly came to the rescue. Richard managed to persuade the team, several of which were local, that their monthly group buying meetings in Bristol should be convened on a Monday morning, rather than midweek. It was a win-win decision all round; a civilised start to the working week for the team and an opportunity for Richard and Samantha to extend their weekends together.

Christmas 1975 provided the first conflict of domestic interests. Richard, thinking like a man, hadn't even considered the consequences of not being at his parents' family table on the 25th but of course Samantha had... He also had no idea that the two most important ladies in his life were in consultation; indeed, in cahoots. Richard, therefore, at his mother's discretion, was despatched to Devon – Samantha in turn would travel north for the annual D'Arcy New Year's Eve party.

Their first formal outing as a couple was the occasion of her sailing club's annual prize giving ball at the Royal Hotel in late October. For the commodore's table, it was indeed a family affair. This year it was to be extra special. Roland was stepping away from the role he had held – owned – for the past five years.

Richard cleaned up well. A revelation in black tie, his appearance was augmented by a stylish haircut and his signature bushy sideboards trimmed to ear lobe level.

But it was Samantha in her figure-hugging emerald backless gown who stole the show. Adding to the occasion of that evening she glided down the Chisholme stairway in full-blown Hollywood style to join her man and her brothers for pre-ball drinks. Henry and latest girlfriend Gael, a petite brunette and fellow architect, were there. Hilary too. Adrienne gave Samantha a close contest in the glamour stakes. Penny and Jonny had also travelled down for the occasion; Richard and Jonny, as newly crowned national champions, were guests of honour.

The occasion also marked Hilary and Richard's first face-to-face since their infamous encounter at the championship. However, and under the combined sanction of the girls, any fireworks which could potentially erupt would, they were warned, be very damp squibs.

Okay, Richard and Hilary's developing relationship would never be cosy; but their combined maturity ensured that it would at least be polite. They shared a private pint; thin apologies were issued, and accepted.

If truth be told it was probably Richard's machinations, ably assisted by a mischievous Jonny, that saw Hilary completely rat-arsed by the end of the evening. It was an evening dominated by numerous toasts to Roland. Samantha was suspicious, but old Roland knew perfectly well what had happened.

'You pair are worth a-watching,' he said, with a glint in his eye. Poor Hilary; but Richard felt no guilt, and if his future brother-in-law suspected he never ever said…

Their first Christmas and New Year gathering came and went in something of a whirlwind. Samantha's resolution to revisit her memories of growing up in nearby Chester amounted to one rainy day out in the seasonally bitter weather. Her time in the north was mostly spent around the roaring fire, bonding with Richard's mum, his elder sister and her two daughters. She had become especially fond of his two brothers.

Jean, the eldest of the children at forty-one and tall like her father, was a long-serving geography and religious education teacher at the local grammar school. With her husband Iain, they had two daughters, nineteen-year-old Vicky and Andrea, seventeen. Iain had recently been laid off after twenty-three years in transport management. He had only just secured a factory job locally. He was quick to announce that whilst it may not be the most illustrious or best-paid position, it was probably the best Christmas present he had ever had.

The eldest of the brothers was John, thirty-eight, who had followed his father into accountancy. He held down a fairly senior position in a Manchester-based practice. He and his wife Gillian, together with their three, Artie, sixteen and Tom and Molly, twelve and ten, lived a comfortable existence in Stockport. John was a golfer. Gillian lived for her drama group.

Number three brother Russell, thirty-seven, was an art teacher. His vocation for the priesthood had been short-lived. He remained resolutely single. He lived and worked in East London, Hackney, many miles from the family home, much to his mother's anxiety.

As youngsters of similar age, Mrs D'Arcy explained to Samantha, John and Russell had fought each other tooth and nail. She went on to confide that at times it was she who would use the strap to separate them – 'For their own good, of course, dear.'

'Whether it was age or marriage or godfather-ship, or just being away from home, they have all become very close. And' – her voice became a whisper – 'maybe someday Russell will find his match; I do hope it's a girl.' Samantha, with dropped jaw, noticed a twinkle in her eye. She also noticed a strong similarity running through all of the D'Arcy siblings; the eyebrows and fine noses and of course the immaculate teeth. The teeth, she noted, were very much a paternal feature. In stature they resembled their mother – petite upright and poised. Samantha dreamed that her children would combine these traits. Richard was his mother's son.

With Richard now based in Bristol, their relationship was developing onto a more easily managed schedule. He quickly moved from a city centre flat to a mid-terraced two-bedroom house on the outskirts. It came complete with a garage – or to Richard's way of thinking, a shed – off a shared rear access lane. His Ford Cortina remained at the mercy of the elements, parked on the main road, while the sailboat got the first call on the shed, the 'boat' shed.

Contrary to accepted wisdom, for Richard and Samantha it was proximity that made the heart grow fonder. Now that the distance between them amounted to little more than a neighbourhood drive, it became crystal clear that the obvious next step would be to cut this to zero. They moved in together.

The summer of '78 saw Mr and Mrs D'Arcy exit from a Devon catholic church. Samantha was led up the aisle by a frail but determined father. Having seen his daughter safely and happily married, Roland passed away the following year after a short illness.

The terrace was replaced by a Weston-super-Mare semi. Richard quickly realised the benefits this partnership provided; he was not only to share his life with a beautiful wife, but had acquired a female crew for his rehabilitated mistress, and, he gained a sea view; 'More of a glimpse,' Richard would eventually concede.

His sailboat no longer needed to be hidden away in a dingy shed. Rigged, she was parked proudly within the local sailing club's compound –Richard and Samantha wasted no time in engaging with the local marine life.

The following year value was added to their family membership at the club. Another potential crew member arrived – eight pounds and five ounces of baby boy Roland, the first of three children. Having transferred from Torquay to the local cottage hospital, the new Mrs D'Arcy was now nursing part-time, three days a week. Otherwise she divided her hectic domestic life between her now high-flying husband – Richard's commercial life had continued apace – and their rapidly growing-up family.

Summer hours were spent with like-minded parents at the sailing club. Together they organised the junior activities, and her involvement within the club-scene broadened. Enriched and beguiled, she found herself stepping up the committee ladder. She was eventually to follow in her father's footsteps, becoming the club's first *lady* commodore.

Richard's leisure time had been seriously depleted. It was a sacrifice; one of the demands of commercial life. But in spite of the frequent battles he was fighting, he always made time to support his first lady. He never complained. In fact he was reassured, because after the birth of their third child, Susanna, he at last would be forever sure of the commodore's daughter's identity. Samantha never missed an opportunity to remind him.

Chapter Twenty-six

Capsize and Recovery

Richard had risen steadily through the ranks of the company. A directorship transferred him permanently to head office and ultimately, at the age of thirty-eight, he was invited to join the main board. He had become something of a whiz in the art of procurement.

He had also headed up an acquisition team. This group was responsible for the further expansion of the company. It had developed into a six-site operation across Great Britain, Ireland and near Europe. Of course in doing so, it had itself become the target of equally large, or larger, global competitors. Life was good for Richard and his fellow board members.

In the years following, however, there developed something of gulf between his ambitious expansionist outlook, and his fellow directors' contentment to remain safe and consolidated. In a marketplace which had and continued to change before their eyes, he, now managing director, frequently found himself and his plans frustrated and seriously at odds with those of his colleagues.

Around the table he had sensed an advancing pressure group for consolidation. Negativity and self-protection, it seemed to Richard, permeated every meeting. It had become a running sore of confrontation. So when it came to one final vote, Richard D'Arcy crucially found himself almost completely isolated.

It was during a period of domestic distraction; he had just buried his father and this was followed several months later with the news that Hilary had been fatally injured in a foggy motorway pile-up. With his attention fixed on his grieving mother and the family circles, especially Samantha, his brother in law and Adrianne, it was a tough time all round. Certainly Richard D'Arcy's focus was not entirely on matters of business.

Whether it was opportunistic but in an instant, a new dynamic was created. To Richard's absolute horror their company became the European arm of an American conglomerate.

Three of the elders and two newish directors walked away with sizeable handshakes. Richard, together with the production director, the director of European sales and the company secretary opted to remain onboard. They accepted a brief to guide this new and predominately Stateside board through the eccentricities, subtleties and complexities of European business. It was in many ways a train-crash-in-waiting.

Only one year and eleven months into the Anglo-US partnership, Richard D'Arcy found himself quite alone. Some months earlier the production supremo had given way to another Yank. This was mirrored not long after when Samuel Pennington, a founding father of the company, stepped down. Apart from Josh Lewis, the sales guy who the Yanks had eating out of the palms of their hands, Richard D'Arcy really was the last man standing. Samuel, whom he regarded not only as his wisest friend, but ultimately his protector, had cited recurring health issues. Richard, however, was fairly sure that he was a just a beaten man. More months crawled by and the rising tide of boardroom battles claimed its final scalp. The D'Arcy era had exhaled its final sigh: his managing directorship was no more!

After a series of head-to-head and frequently ill-tempered disagreements on policy, it had all erupted. He had remained resolute about his workers' rights, their contracts of employment. But in a global market, according to the Yanks, this was not a key issue – an attitude Richard simply could not countenance. He was in disbelief. The company was on the cusp of the first ever all-out strike, while they blindly forced forward plans for confrontation. But even at the eleventh hour, Richard's proven leadership credentials saved the day. A personal intervention allowed disruption to be avoided and the plant returned to edgy normality. But output inefficiencies, and papered over cracks in product quality together with customers claims against shoddy goods, were increasingly on the agenda.

The dominance of the US board had finally played its merciless card. Richard and his cautious, some would say forensic, style of leadership became completely counter to their brasher approach to business. Already wounded, his vulnerability had been laid bare. A principled man, he found himself forced into a 'back me or sack me' confrontation. It was a critical miscalculation; he taken one leap too far. He should have seen it coming, but he didn't.

His world crashed down around him, ironically on a frosty but bright-blue-skied Monday morning in Bristol; and following his departure, the shock-waves which emanated from the top quickly reached the gutters of the various shop floors. Customers and suppliers alike revisited their connections with the troubled company. Time being no friend to loyalty, industry marched on.

He was left devastated, mentally and physically. For many months Samantha's natural caring instinct was put heavily to the test. Creating an environment for a fallen leader was not going to be a straightforward task. A life in which self-esteem, confidence, and most of all pride had been wrenched away, could not be rebuilt quickly. It became a dark time, the best part of a year. Richard often thought of Dave Gilmour, and indeed felt the pressures he must have been under. His unexpected early retirement threw up many complications, not least financial.

He worried; but he possessed a deep-down resilience, and he knew he could count on Samantha's unfailing love and support. She possessed, he discovered, strengths long closeted and untapped.

Reminiscent of when he had put his folks through the wringer, Richard's deepening gloom unexpectedly shattered one evening. While slumped, unshaven, in front of the television, watching nothing in particular, he shocked the gathering by sitting bolt upright and declaring:

'Enough! Enough of this shit; those bastards aren't going to get away that easy!'

Samantha, young Roland, and Richard junior stared at him in disbelief. Susanna was asleep.

He dialled Gerry Freestone's number there and then. An appointment with Baxter, Bell & Freestone was arranged for lunchtime the following day. A legal team was put together.

A catalogue of brutal legal skirmishes finally concluded in court; it had not been pretty. Richard's 'across the pond' colleagues had again miscalculated, and it had cost them dear. They were totally unaware just how tenacious – vicious, when the occasion demanded – their previous leader could be when riled. With costs, his pay-off, and the release of various bonuses due, he and the family were financially more comfortable. The blackness had eased to grey. He even dropped his separate case against the 'sales guy' for defamation of character. His storm clouds had parted. They revealed a brightness and an opportunity to build a new life. The D'Arcy's found themselves comfortable enough to finally bury his business corpse, and retire to Devon. A family harmonised again, they submerged themselves in the benefits of a mild coastal climate.

With the blinding fog finally lifted, he realised that he had the perfect opportunity to revisit his hitherto clandestine interest in architecture. They took a rented place in Brixham until such time as they could find and secure a suitable building site which overlooked Torbay – their long-held dream. The call of Devon had proved stronger for Samantha than the friendships she and the children had developed in and around Weston. Richard was neutral, but attracted by the prospect of building his own house.

A reinvented and revitalised ex-leader of industry, together with his brother-in-law Henry, he proceeded to do just that – doing much of the labouring himself. The site was on a gentle slope looking southeast. It commanded a magnificent view out over Torbay and across into Dorset. It sat well with the landscape.

The style of house was – indeed had been for some time – fixed in Richard's head. It would be a distinctive modern property. Low-rise, backed if possible into the hillside. It would feature lots of glass and a generous veranda. It would be contemporary and bright. It would include a battery of boys' toys, but above all it would be homely.

In consultation and, for the most part, agreement with his wife, images – loads of them – were created, blended and outlined in sketches. Henry converted them into formal drawings… which Richard and Samantha would regularly modify. Henry was a patient architect.

The move re-ignited the flame of competitive sailing for Richard D'Arcy. Sometime prior to moving he had sold his second 'mistress', the ex-Dave Gilmore boat. He had been gradually moving away from the dinghy-racing scene, but in doing so it had created a profound and unsettling void in his new life. Of course, supporting his family in the rapidly expanding youth regatta scene was, for the most part, an enormous pleasure. But it wasn't allowing *him* any personal time afloat. Okay, he finally reasoned, the kids need me Friday to Sunday, but aside from the usual demands of family life, I have the rest of the week to myself.

Richard had perfected the habit of not conforming to the norm. His expected move into the local Dragon sailing scene was aborted after several conversations with Jonny. Even though his mate was successful in private dentistry, he felt that it would be an extravagance. Jonny had long since taken a different turn, and for that very reason. He preferred instead to waste – in Richard's words – his accumulated wealth chasing wee white balls around the topography of Scotland. To keep his hand in at the sailing, Richard had eased himself into the local club scene. He joined the crew of a fellow member's yacht for local events, allowing him the opportunity to learn how yachts work – in principle, he soon discovered, not unlike dinghies: his experience would stand him in good stead.

Crewing also helped greatly with his research. That research finally led him to acquire an elderly, and very tired, 30ft. long glass-fibre offshore racing yacht. Oh boy, he thought, is she tired. He wondered if he'd done the right thing but undaunted, he immersed himself in 'the project.' She was a Nicholson 303, and she was undeniably sleek. *She has lots of potential. She's in dire need of a makeover. More like a re-build...* But by doing most of the labouring himself costs, he decided, could be kept under control. Enthused and reinvigorated, he became quite engrossed. His time served on his club mate's yacht had of course amassed for him a mountain of information. It also provided him with invaluable contacts, who opened doors to skilled people for those tricky jobs that he couldn't manage himself. For a start, he had a seized bloody engine to sort...

From the owner's point of view, having Richard aboard was like winning the Pools every weekend. His tactical ability and general race mentality had never left him. Various victories followed. It was thought of as a win-win scenario.

After two years – two winters and a summer – his new 'mistress' was ready for the water. If he thought that this was a cheap way of getting afloat, Richard soon discovered that he had been kidding himself. Samantha never knew, or so she claimed, the extent of the outgoings. The exercise provided excellent therapy. A barrow-load of previously unaccounted for equipment plus the cost of cosmetic treatments easily blew his original budget. Worse, he had also opted to upgrade the entire sail wardrobe, and replace that engine. True, with help he had fitted it himself; well, he had to admit the 'help' was ninety-nine percent Dave Gilmore.

Richard had kept in contact with Dave. Notwithstanding their many on-the-water debacles, their friendship strengthened over time. In many ways, it had been Richard's earlier support and his business guidance that had allowed Dave to sort himself – and his boatyard – out. Dave, in turn, was always there for Richard. Together with a new lady, ironically another Sally, he had created a platform on which he built a cleaner, more forward-looking lifestyle.

He and Sally sold the yard, now in good shape, and together they moved inland to Windermere. He took up a position of maintenance manager with one of the ferry operators on the great lake. The money wasn't great, but set against the stress levels he had previously submitted himself to, it was a penny from heaven.

Sally was a successful representative for a chemical company – resins and fibreglass. That's how they met; he was a customer. Together they made a tight and settled partnership. So when Richard's mechanical S.O.S. came through, there was no hesitation. Dave's tools were loaded into the boot of Sally's red Vauxhall Cavalier estate. Richard and Samantha, in turn, enjoyed many visits to the Lake District. When there, they divided their time between the water and the hills, and, of course, the Gilmour's hospitality.

For the long-awaited launch day, Jonny and Penny, plus their two girls, were in attendance. The occasion was made the sweeter by the presence of the youngest D'Arcy, baby Susanna. The yacht's hull was again a gleaming white, but now it had contrasting grey waterline stripes and a black bottom. In a late morning sun she gleamed like a showroom model. Samantha did the honours – champagne.

With all the boys on board she slid gracefully down the harbour slipway. It was a still, balmy morning. Perfect for the launch, but a complete absence of wind meant that her maiden voyage was to be a test drive for her new engine. It started first time; Richard sweated, Dave didn't. By noon she was tethered to her mooring. The crew made their way to shore courtesy of the club's boatman. The nine-strong party, plus various helpers, marked a successful launch with a celebration lunch. *Moonlighter* lay there majestically afloat, silent, glued on a mirrored seascape.

The following day allowed them to break out the new white sails and, of course, the obligatory orange and purple spinnaker. Dave steered while Jonny, and especially Richard, ran around the deck like demented seagulls. Both families enjoyed a proper sail. It was gloriously typical of the bay, but all too quickly it was a mad dash ashore. The Dubois clan needed a lift back to the airport for their return to Edinburgh. Alas for their girls, it was back to school on Monday.

In their maturing years Richard and Samantha immersed themselves in the local yachty scene. Their children, Roland, Richard jnr. and 'baby' Susanna, whilst improving their collective skills level afloat, each enjoyed pride-engendering academic success on dry land.

Roland went on to carve a successful career in accountancy. Richard jnr. followed in his grandfather's architectural footsteps, but in Europe. Susanna, being something of a home bird, went into the tourism business and based herself in Devon.

In due course, the family grew; five grandchildren hove into view, and Richard and Samantha enjoyed every second of it. They also found time to cover many miles afloat, cruising and racing in their beloved yacht. They combed the Devon coastline round to Dartmouth, their favourite stopover. For extended holidays they often navigated the Channel and submerged themselves in the Brittany scene: St. Malo was, and would remain, their favourite European port of call. Following Hilary's death, Adrianne had relocated not far from the port. The D'Arcy's never lost contact with her.

But while cruising *Moonlighter* provided many hours of stress free sailing, for Richard, winning the occasional race still fired his nautical passion like nothing else. Watching his children and grandchildren doing the same came a close second. He felt no guilt over this modicum of selfishness.

Chapter Twenty-seven

Wind-shifts and Shadow Chasing

A nudge; a gentle hand on the shoulder, and a voice from far
above…

'Er, Richard.' 'Dad.' 'Richard, old boy.' Richard D'Arcy was
being winched back from his memories with a sympatric shake.
David, Susanna's husband, had been despatched by his wife. From
the cockpit, her impatience threatened to override his son-in-law's
quiet tone… 'Dad.' Susanna's impatience won the day, she
continued;

'What's keeping you David? Look, I need both of you up here.'
She tended to become a little elongated in times of rising stress.

'What's all the fuss about, dear?' her father, at last, answered, a
little surprised.

David, in the meantime, had quietly and sure-footedly, made his way back, to position himself, among the crew on deck. They were all lined shoulder to shoulder, sitting, legs dangling over the windward side of the healed yacht. The breeze had indeed filled in. He clutched his tablet; a new toy, a hand-held navigation station. He punched in a new series of numbers and recommenced his calculations.

Richard, his arms now resting on the sides of the companionway, looked around, still a bit sleepy-eyed.

'Where are we exactly? Jeez, it's bright up here. I say, the breeze has filled in nicely.'

'Dad,' said Susanna, pointedly addressing her father while passing over the binoculars. 'See that big blue yacht, that one, the Swan, way ahead?' Richard, now standing steady, legs apart, in the cockpit, nodded. Then she placed her free hand on her father's shoulder, turning him to face aft. 'Look, see those three smaller ones astern, especially that red Sonata?'

Richard nodded again, letting the bins hang on their cord around his neck. He didn't speak.

'Well, David reckons that on corrected time we are at best, level pegging with more or less all of them. I think that he was humouring me.' David was the navigator. He did the hard sums. These he then translated into the relative speeds of both larger and smaller yachts. Into real time – corrected time. Sometimes they exposed facts that would have been better left unseen, or said. Richard, who remained quiet could remember one particular incident where Jonny really bugged him, replying to what he had considered a reasonable question with, '...I'm only the muscle'. Of course a bit of anger, he thought, can make you focus.

Aye, that was a day and a half.

'Dad! What will we do? Come on, help me.' Susanne was agitated. 'I'm really, really, sorry to have wakened you. You looked so cosy down there. But I need you to fire up that old treasure chest of a racing brain of yours if we're ever going to win this race. We really need to win this one. Sweet dreams, by the way?'

'Just thinking of your Mum, dear, and of course sailing with Jonny all those years ago.' He smiled. 'So; so let's see, where we are first of all...'

Samantha had passed away some two years before, following an illness. Then Jonny. It had been less than a year; a massive stroke, without any warning, and it had robbed Richard of his best mate. The last couple of years had seen Richard weathering difficult times.

He had been forced to look on helplessly while the woman to whom he was so devoted just wasted away in front of him. Still the most beautiful creature he had ever set eyes on, the cancer had taken its toll. Not just on Samantha, but on the entire family. Richard could only comfort her while the Macmillan nurses regulated and dulled her pain.

It seemed like only yesterday: after showering, Samantha drew Richard's attention to a single mole which was particularly itchy. He thought of that morning; he thinks of it in every moment of every present day. He remembered her exact words. Each word, each syllable. Her expression. She knew she was in trouble...

'Oh scratch me darling, I'm so itchy, and not with that toothbrush.' joked Samantha, as she emerged wriggling, trying to cool the sensation by rubbing herself on the edge of the cubicle frame.

Drawing blood, Richard's immediate thoughts were that he had scratched her too vigorously. But after a closer inspection – she looking on over her shoulder, and via the bathroom mirror – they both agreed that one mole looked a bit crusty and menacingly dark. En route to the local surgery a day or so later, they were both unusually quiet.

She had her suspicions. She was expecting the worst. Richard remained anxious, for her. He had sensed every wave of her concern. The resulting excision biopsy confirmed that it was an advanced nodular melanoma with secondary cancers. It was the worst possible scenario.

The bravery of Samantha in running her everyday life over the following months was inspirational. Initially Richard was a mess, but drawing on her strength he became progressively more able take the strain.

She was eventually and mercifully taken early on a wet windswept September morning. Samantha was surrounded by her family. As the breaking sun became smothered within the greyness of the horizon, her grip on Richard's hand loosened at 05:35 hours.

The eldest, Roland, had been preparing for his move to the New York office, his wife and family soon to follow. Richard jnr. and his emerging family were resident in France – had been for some years. Without Susanna, who had recently married David, it had suddenly become an empty and a quiet house. It had reverted to just that: a structure of bricks and mortar hanging on a cold steel skeleton. Its heart of idyllic family life ripped from the foundations.

Every tick of time which passed thereafter resembled that grey soulless morning. It also reminded Richard of when he and Jonny first launched *Satisfaction* into the Long Lake. This time around, however, there was to be no lifting breeze to guide him out of absolute despair. Sunlight could not break through the dark clouds that had consumed him. The view over Torbay that he and Sam had so much cherished had been indelibly tarnished. It signalled instead a life destined to be forever shrouded in mist.

Moonlighter was laid up and eventually sold. Susanna's husband brokered the deal. Richard remained anchored deep in depression. He had no interest in life, never mind boats. A broken man, he simply could not function without the countenance of his life partner.

Regardless of the loving support he received from his children, his circles of friends, and of course Jonny and Dave Gilmore who comforted and counselled him, he remained buried in despair and grief. He did occasionally succumb to his daughter's constant badgering. He comforted himself in her smile; it reminded him of happier times. She was sure that each time she got him afloat, the occasion planted in him an inkling of light. It was a slow process.

Slowly, at least superficially, he came to terms with the situation. Going afloat onboard his daughter's shapely 22-foot, red and white yacht, offered him a modicum of therapy. Richard gradually eased back into touch with people. His sense of community was rebuilding. The seeds of normal life, or as normal as a life could be, were sprouting.

Being introduced to the world of golf by his son-in-law provided a diversion. It prised him away from his usual haunts and memories afloat with his wife. It of course presented a perfect opportunity for Jonny to mock him.

The grieving process is long and drawn but sometimes it can act as an aid in facing up to an array of issues, as he was soon to discover.

All the D'Arcy family were devastated when the news of Jonny's sudden death came through. But it was Richard who found strength. He immediately formed himself into the rock on which

Penny was able to lean. She was an only child; her parents long departed. Her family circle around Cumbria was sparse. He, without a second's delay, had flown up to Edinburgh to stand beside her. With unrelenting energy and unsparing charity, he more or less single-handedly organised the wake, the funeral, the service – spoke eloquently of his friendship with Jonny – and thereafter helped to put in order her personal affairs. He commented repeatedly, and indeed convinced himself, than Sam would have wanted him involved.

Jonny's death had injected, nay shocked life back into Richard. Thereafter, Penny and Richard developed a close platonic relationship. She remained in Scotland, and, with her daughters married and living abroad, she moved further north to a comfortable cottage overlooking Loch Leven.

Richard had also moved. He gave up the hillside site, and after much persuasion, moved into a 'grandpa' flat annexed onto Susanna and David's house in Paignton.

'Oh Dad, you're so cool.' Susanna kissed her dad on his forehead and announced: 'Come on then, it's not only your experience but Jonny's divine guidance we need to sail us to the finish of this race.' The rest of the crew just smiled. They felt that her tactics would have been more appropriate to the last chance salon.

The breeze, albeit unstable, had remained. It was shifting some five degrees back and forth, from port to starboard. Richards's overgrown eyebrows were twitching. Susanna eased her dad up onto the windward side of *Mistress*. Just like him in his day, Susanna had become a leading helm. Indeed she and David were defending the title they won at last year's regatta. This time, however, it was in their newly acquired Élan 333, a 34-foot cruiser/racer – David was part of the London financial scene. With father by her side, snugly nestled into the yacht's aft guard rail, Susanna's confidence was returning.

'You know something, dear?' Richard said.

'What?' She was concentrating hard, eking out every available knot of speed. The clock ticked away.

'This is uncanny. This is almost exactly how Jonny and me saw the last leg of our race.'

'Yes Dad. That was then, this is now. Have you any positives to offer other than chasing a shadow...?' She was off again. Up until now, Richard had ignored her uneasiness, but sensed that it was time to act.

'Okay dear, let's just take a breath. Let's look at the conditions.' He went quiet, as did she.

'Tell you what...' He paused. 'Tack the boat round and drive off in that direction. Go on do it, trust your old dad.'

She looked at him. She was unsure. But she nevertheless made the call. A leap of faith?

The crew spontaneously sprung into action. Everyone knew their job. In a flash, *Mistress* was making waves, now close onto the wind, out towards the port side of the course. After some twenty minutes' sailing, Richard, with the salty spray caking on his craggy face, directed his daughter to tack back again. She did – they were laying the finishing line. David was frantically pressing the buttons on his tablet, he had been for some time. An earlier grin had been transformed into wide smile as they crossed the finishing line.

'How did they do that?' someone said. The whole crew was a-gasp, reflecting on that final dash.

It had been a unique day. Her dad's crystal-clear memory of the very race course where he and his lifelong friend had won their first national title, had come to the surface at exactly the right moment. It was so very many years ago, but the day had allowed him to re-live the race in all its colour and excitement. In truth, it had uneased him a bit; it was all a little spooky. Glancing skywards, both Susanna and her father had the same private thought. They never concurred.

Richard had not only demonstrated his ability to understand the vagaries of the local weather systems but delicately guided his daughter through to the end of this vital race. The title was indeed defended – by a mere one and a quarter seconds. Looking at his wristwatch, Richard realised that they had been sailing almost three hours. Then he said quietly:

'It's amazing how much of your life you can spend shadow chasing.'

Susanna, now also smiling broadly, motioned for her father to take the wheel. As he moved into position, she bounced forward to embrace her husband. The crew applauded. Richard smiled.

ENDS

Glossary of Terms

Sailing Speak!

Afloat Refers to the sailing and racing which takes place on the water, including the race area.

Ashore Refers to the pre- and post-racing environment; the organisation, the club and the social functions.

Aft The rear or back section of a boat.

Après-sail The social aspect of competition.

Brasso A brand of liquid polish favoured for the shining of silver cups and trophies.

Bear off A change in direction; when a boat is steered away from the wind direction

Bent on A nautical term for attaching sails onto a boat's spars.

Bias On this occasion, 'line bias'. In sailboat racing a starting (or finishing) line is laid by means of anchoring a vessel in a designated area. At right angles to the prevailing wind a buoy anchored some distance away. If this (imaginary) line between the vessel's mast and the buoy is not at a right angles the line is therefore biased towards one end or the other.

Block The common nautical name for a pulley, or wheel, over which a rope is pulled.

Boom The horizontal 'pole' or spar onto which the mainsail's lower or bottom edge is attached.

Close-hauled A sailing boat cannot sail directly into the wind but with her sails fully trimmed in she can achieve in general terms approx. 45 degrees to the wind – this is referred to as; 'close-hauled'.

Capsize When a sailboat is blown over, to an extent that its mast is horizontal with the water, and its cockpit awash – it is then capsized.

Cockpit The inside or working area of a boat.

Centreboard A long flat retractable keel usually made of wood. It restricts the sideways movement of a sailboat when dropped down into the vertical plane.

Centreboard casing A narrow box fitted along the centre-line of the dinghy in which the centreboard is housed when retracted.

Commodore One of the highest offices a member of a boat/sailing/yacht club can attain.

Chandlery A retail establishment which specialises in the sale of nautical equipment, clothing and accessories.

Class Refers to groupings of similar or identical boats where owners come together in association, normally to compete on an equal basis; for example, the Dragon class, the GP14 class, the Laser class etc.

Chart Put simply this is the AA map of the sea. Charts are available normally from a chandlery shop.

Crew Refers to the person positioned in the forward section of the boat/dinghy as opposed to the helmsperson who steers the boat. Crew can also be used in the plural to describe all personnel on board.

Cleat A mechanical device with serrated spring-loaded jaws used to grip and hold ropes.

Cove line A painted line, a few inches deep, located just under a boat's gunwale. It will contrast with the hull colour.

Downwind As opposed to upwind or close-hauled. When a boat is sailing away from the wind she is sailing 'downwind' or 'off-wind'. This includes when the wind is blowing squarely over the boat's side, known as reaching. When the wind is blowing directly over the stern, the sailboat is 'running' downwind.

Deck head The ceiling of a yacht's cabin.

Dinghy A small boat with a centreboard, normally launched off the beach or bank.

Dinghy park A dedicated area where dinghies are parked or stored when ashore.

Dragon A classic 30 ft long racing yacht of Scandinavian design.

Fitting A general term used to describe any of the array of cleats, fairleads and blocks etc. required in the trimming of the sails.

Fleet A term to describe a group of sailing boats.

Gybe Occurs when sailing down wind. When a sailboat changes course and the wind which was blowing over, say, the port side is now coming over the starboard side, causes the mainsail to be blown across – suddenly – to the opposite side of the sailboat. Gybes in windy conditions are dramatic. The energy which is generated during the manoeuvre is the commonest cause of capsizing in sailing dinghies.

Gybe mark On most race courses a turning mark is anchored in such a position that it forces the fleet to execute a gybe turn. In windy conditions – 15 mph plus – this area is commonly referred to as 'the sailor's graveyard'.

Halyard A rope used to haul up a sail.

Helmsman A person who steers the boat. Also referred to as: helm, skipper, and lady helmsman or helmsperson.

Heading(or veering) When the wind shifts direction.

Headed In sailboat racing you are headed when the wind shifts and the angle of 'close-hauled' increases.

Jib A triangular sail set forward or located in front of the mast.

Keel An appendage fixed under a yacht. Normally cast in iron, steel or lead. Its purpose is to balance the load on the sails, keep the boat upright and prevent it sailing sideways or off to 'leeward'. NB: A keel is generally non-retractable, unlike the centreboard.

Leeward The side of the boat from which the wind exits; as opposed to 'windward'.

Mistress Refers to the boat! It is slang pretty much, in the 'golf widow' idiom…

Mainsail Attached to the mast and boom, it is normally the largest sail on the boat. It also carries a registration number (sail number) and normally a class emblem.

Mainsheet A rope rigged for trimming mainsails. Such ropes are referred to as sheets. Ropes used for hoisting sails are referred to as 'halyards'.

Mainsheet cleat A mechanical jawed device for gripping the mainsheet thus leaving hands of the helmsperson free.

Off-wind See 'downwind'. This term covers many angles of sailing other than 'close-hauled' or 'onthewind'.

Port (as opposed to 'starboard') The left side of the boat. When the wind is blowing over the left side of the boat she is on 'port tack'.

Port tack See above. Port tack is the 'give way' tack. When sailboats meet, the one on port tack must alter course to avoid a collision.

Planning In windy conditions lightweight sailing dinghies, like speed boats, plane. The experienced helm can, like a surfer, steer across and down a wave to extract speed, way above that which a dinghy designed for – get it wrong and the result is a (spectacular) capsize!

Ready about When sailing 'close-hauled' this is the common command or warning when the helm is planning to change direction, or execute a tack.

Regatta An organised event in which sailing (& rowing) boats/yachts compete..

Reaching leg When the wind is squarely coming across the side of a sailboat she is said to be reaching.See also; off-wind.

Racing rules As in any competitive sport, competition is governed by rules. Sailing 'rule books' are obtainable from either a chandlery shop or a national authority such as the Royal Yachting, or Irish Sailing Association.

Starboard When the wind is blowing in over the right side of the boat she is on starboard tack. The word 'starboard' is also the common hailing 'warning cry' when sailboats meet.

Starboard tack Starboard tack is the 'right of way tack' when sailboats meet. The boat on starboard however must allow the port-tacked boat time and room to take avoiding action. This also applies in racing conditions.

Stern The back of a boat.

Sails Sails are the means of propulsion. They are constructed using special cloth cut into aerofoil shapes, very much like aeroplane wings. Air (wind) is directed across them and in conjunction with the keel/centreboard move the boat forward through the water.

Spinnaker A balloon-like sail, usually multi-coloured, and hoisted only when 'off-wind'. This sail traps more air, propelling a sailboat through the water faster.

Sit out A term used to describe the action of the crew when balancing the pressure on the sails when levering the sailboat upright.

Shifting wind The wind is never still and when its direction changes the sailor refers to this a 'wind shift'. In land-lubber parlance it could be referred to as; chasing shadows.

Sail their own race In a sailboat race competitors can get locked into groups and get so immersed that an overall advantage can be lost to another competitor choosing to break away into clear air/wind –'sailing their own race'.

Slipway A hard, usually concrete, path leading from the dinghy park out into the water. It is constructed specially for the launching of boats.

Tack To change direction – see also port & starboard tack. Also, a 'covering' tack is when the leading sailboat changes direction to position herself directly upwind of another competitor, thus creating a 'wind shadow' which deprives that (covered) boat of clear wind. The covered boat would then normally tack away. A 'crash' tack is a 'last-moment' avoiding action – usually by the port-tacked boat – when boats are on collision course. The more experienced crews in dinghy racing have evolved a slicker and faster method of tacking. This is known as the 'roll tack'. The sailboat, normally a lightweight dinghy, is physically rolled though the wind using minimal rudder movement, then with much athleticism, levered upright onto the opposite tack. Done properly the boat will actually accelerate, gaining precious positioning. Could be likened to a rally car going into a corner on opposite lock!

Tiller A stick attached to the rudder projecting into the cockpit, which allows the boat to be steered.

Tiller extension Utilising a universal joint another 'stick' is attached to the tiller allowing the helm to steer from a position sitting out on the side deck of the boat.

Toe straps Lengths of [seat belt] webbing attached to the cockpit floor of a dinghy under which, the crew hook their feet to assist in 'sitting out'.

Transom The flat stern of a boat. Sailors sometimes use it as slang to describe the rear-end of a person of the opposite sex...

Tonnage A common nautical slang for a vessel – 'new tonnage' therefore refers to a new boat for the owner.

Team racing A specialist sector of competitive sailing where six identical dinghies – three on each side – are raced. The team with the best aggregate score wins. It remains a very popular university pastime.

Veering (or heading) When the wind shifts direction.

Windward The side of a boat over which the wind blows in.

Wind-shift When direction of wind changes.

Yardarm The horizontal or angled pole on a flagstaff from which flags are flown. Also known as an (upper) boom onto which a sail is bent.

OTHER TITLES BY THE SAME AUTHOR:

THE BIG EVENT

The 'best practice' regatta planning and management manual. A free download, available from the author's website; www.tnjobling.com.

CHAMPIONS & HIGH ACHIEVERS

A historical listing of the great and the good [sailors] from East Antrim Boat Club in Northern Ireland, from its 1950 inauguration on Larne Lough, to the year 2013.

Look out for other titles by TN Jobling: Females & Fast Cars, Arthur's Dead, among others...